The Six-Foot Bonsai

The Six-Foot Bonsai

A SOUL LOST IN THE LAND
OF THE RISING SUN

Stacy Gleiss

Cover Photo: (c) Nexus7@Dreamstime.com

www.thesixfootbonsai.com
thesixfootbonsai@gmail.com

ISBN: 0692773134
ISBN 13: 9780692773130

The life history of the individual is first and foremost an accommodation to the patterns and standards traditionally handed down in his community.

Ruth Benedict, *The Patterns of Culture*, 1934

Contents

Preface

WE RECEIVE ALL KINDS OF input from the world, much of it haphazard and circumstantial. Everything we take in is based on the contexts of place, time, and our limited ability to distinguish what is truly relevant from a continual barrage of sensual stimuli. Many people (myself included) are drawn to exotic cultures, lured into thinking this or that art or custom is simply a unique expression, appearing somehow from within a vacuum, divorced from that which goes on behind paper doors, so to speak. It's important, wherever you are, to be aware of these connections and to understand that all cultures are man-made systems of value, created and judged by our limited sensibilities and unworthy of blind followership. There is in fact a true north, an ultimate truth that rises above our own systems. It's our job to identify this and live accordingly, regardless of where we are born and our random exposure.

I threw myself headlong into Japanese culture, knowing very little but latching on because it was so traditionally cool and accepting. It wasn't until I was well along in my Japanese identity transformation that I was exposed to—or perhaps willing to acknowledge—the less savory aspects of the culture. But even so, I hung on and turned a deliberate blind eye.

However, as I began to see more and more weaknesses in Japan's system of values, I gradually began to turn away...but not before extensive damage had been done. And the fallout for our family was anything but random. In fact, it was a product of the culture itself—of Japan's normalization of lolikon (the idolization of young girls) and its historical infatuation with incest (the Japanese islands are said to have been born of a relationship between sibling gods). This experience has radically shaken my trust in cultures established apart from God.

I began recording the events of my Japanese life in 2001 as I left it, when my memories were vivid and clear. But of course my recollections are tainted by my interpretation and views. It should be understood that I love Japan and bear no grudge. With all of the missteps I have made, how can I? To protect the souls still lost, the names of places and people have been altered.

Stacy Gleiss, a.k.a. Bonsai

To my rangers Pink and Blue, may you find the meaning of life early and live joyfully.
To Kent, you are simply the best! Thank you for accepting us—baggage and all.

PART I

Becoming Bonsai

CHAPTER 1

The Strange Pen

DURING WHAT SHOULD HAVE BEEN the sweetest years of my life, I chased moon rabbits and danced with demons as the seed-sowing monkey sat on its haunches and watched. I burned cedar incense from both ends on the altar of culture until there was nothing left but the ashes of my misdirected prayers.

Japan's lore was so intoxicating to me that it seeped into my soul from my first visit there. Without thinking it through, even as a teenager, I began to mimic the quiet, purposeful movements of this ancient culture.

Before long, a five-hundred-year-old seed was planted within me. It germinated in a Japanese hothouse of turmoil—and even after I managed to spring free, those root-bound days of my bonsai years have never left me, and never will.

My life changed the day I received the mechanical pen.

I was sitting in Narita Airport recalling my enchanted summer—intently soaking up what little bit of the culture remained in the bustling international hub. I drew and released each breath slowly, keenly aware that I was taking in my last few doses of the rarified Japanese air.

In my purse were a few mementos from my time there as an exchange student. Each friend who had come to see me off had brought me a gift—everything from a key chain filled with Mt. Fuji lava rocks to photos of our outings together. Everyone, even those who couldn't make it to the airport that day, had signed well-wishes on a piece of paper.

I had saved one box to open last. Sliding my forefinger beneath the wrapping paper, I carefully lifted the gold seal that secured it.

Inside was a lovely silver pen. I pushed the top once, and a blue-tipped shaft appeared. I pushed again and got black. Over and over again I pushed that top, and, seemingly at random, one or another of the three colors would appear.

I asked myself, "Why would the Japanese want to make a pen like this? It's so unlike them to create anything that defies logic."

I spotted a few Caucasian girls nearby, engaged in conversation with a younger Japanese man in a stylish beige suit. Holding the instructions and the pen, I approached the man.

"Excuse me. I don't understand how to use this pen. Can you help me?" I asked.

I was barely able to speak. My throat was sore, and my voice rasped from all of my good-byes and tears.

The man's eyes widened. "*Ohhhh!* You are so tall!"

He took the pen from my outstretched hands and with fairly competent English showed me that tiny shifting weights inside the pen were responsible for the magic. *Mochiron,* I thought—of course. It was Japanese. It was completely logical.

I left the group to continue with the conversation that I had interrupted. I returned to my seat.

Oh, how I dreaded leaving Japan. During my short summer exchange, I had come to love the island nation. It was a place where everything had significance and purpose. There were always logical or spiritual explanations behind objects and actions, and this philosophical view of the world suited me.

I had for as far back as I could remember craved a deeper meaning to life. Nothing—not schoolbooks, family, or religion, as I had been exposed to it—had provided me with a framework that held together my teenage soul the way the Japanese culture seemed to do. I watched the light glint off the pen. Somehow, someway, I would find my place within that structure.

During the flight my dread intensified as I faced the prospect of returning to a place where I was essentially a nobody. I would have no Japanese friends nearby and few resources on which to rely when it came to expanding my knowledge of this intriguing country.

Several rows ahead, a familiar face appeared. There was the man who had explained the pen, leaning up against a row of seats, talking with the same girls he had been chatting up in the terminal. I decided to approach him once more. Maybe I could get some last-minute insights about Japan from him.

As I drew near, I realized that the man was holding a microcassette recorder. I could hear him coaxing the girls to speak into the device.

"Say anything. Come on. I want to study native English sound. Please," he cajoled.

But the girls resisted, burying their faces in their hands to reinforce their refusal. Finally, the man saw me watching and pointed the device toward me.

"My voice is too bad." I waved the recorder away. "I stayed up too late talking with my friends."

The man laughed. "Oh, it's too late! I just recorded!"

I protested in jest, stating that I'd been tricked and asking him to erase what he'd recorded.

"For your lovely voice, I will give you something from my bag." He turned and walked toward the front of the plane. I noticed that he had a slight limp.

When he returned he was holding a folded Japanese fan.

"I have better things in my suitcase, but now I only have my fan. I will sign it for you."

The man opened it with a quick snap of the wrist. Across its pale ocean scene, he scribbled four Chinese characters. Pointing to the first character, he explained, "This means *Chrysanthemum,* the flower."

He pointed again and moved his finger underneath the remaining three characters in succession. "Pond. Right. Man."

"Chrysanthemum Pond Right Man?" I repeated, mystified.

"Yes. My name."

"Right Man is your name? So you are Mr. Right?"

I wondered whether he knew what his name actually meant in English.

"No, I'm Mr. Chrysanthemum Pond," he laughed. "And when I get to America, I will send you something better from my suitcase."

He leaned in, and his cologne was subtle, pleasant. I estimated him to be somewhere in his twenties—perhaps he was a professional of some kind. To complement his business suit, he sported a fancy calculator watch, the likes of which I'd never seen. In addition to being well dressed, he was relatively tall, only a couple of inches shorter than my nearly six-foot stature. He had a kind face and bedroom eyes with heavy, thick lids.

"There's an empty seat next to mine," I invited. "Do you want to sit back here and talk? It's such a long, boring flight to sit alone."

Right Man instantly accepted my invitation and followed me back to my seat. We began our conversation with the basic "getting to know you" topics: our families, where we came from, and what had brought us to this plane trip.

It turned out that Right Man was not a businessman at all but a college student going to Louisiana to study English. His parents and grandmother lived on Sado, a small island in the Sea of Japan. With great enthusiasm he described Sado as some sort of cultural cradle where traditions developed, thrived, and survived, screened from the carnage of WWII and removed from decades of Westernization.

He pulled out a scrap piece of paper and sketched a map to illustrate the location of his home. The island looked to me like a lopsided spool with mountain ranges on both ends and a narrow valley in between.

Our conversation flowed for the next couple of hours, as Right—as he asked me to call him—described in great detail the topography of his homeland, spicing the monologue with explanations of its traditions and delicacies.

As I listened to the man's vivid descriptions, I became increasingly wide eyed. I shared with Right my plans to return to Japan after I graduated from high school and promised I'd make a special effort to travel to Sado.

"Then you must come to my family home and stay." With this pronouncement he began to relax—loosening his necktie and trading his loafers for a pair of the disposable slippers that came with our seats.

As Right Man settled in, I began to talk of my adventures in Tokyo. I pulled out the photos my friends had given me at the airport and handed them to him. Among them were a few additional images—pictures of me with a very special Japanese boy I'd met at a mountain camp, a boy who had said he loved me.

Shuffling through the pictures, Right Man emitted short grunting noises, as though he were evaluating each one. When he came to one particular snapshot, he huffed more loudly.

"What's wrong?" I asked.

Right held up the picture of me leaning into Yasu's shoulder. Pointing directly at my boyfriend, he announced, "This boy is no good."

"What do you mean?" I asked, mildly alarmed.

"I know his type. His hair is colored with some kind of orange dye, isn't it? Good high schools don't allow that. So from this I know he goes to a bad school."

None of my other Japanese friends had any color in their hair. I wasn't sure, but I thought they all seemed smart and studious, so maybe they did go to better schools.

Right thumped the photograph with his forefinger. "Bad school usually means bad parents. Low class. No good."

Where I came from, everyone was pretty much working class. I didn't know any society folks and wondered what he would think of my rather scrappy family. My grandmother had only attended school up to the eighth grade, and my parents were simple.

"Well, I don't care about his school, whether he is rich or poor. I care about whether he's kind."

Right, seeming not to hear what I'd said, continued explaining how to distinguish between good and bad people by their dress and mannerisms. He was essentially suggesting that I was naïve when it came to Japan and that I needed to be careful.

Eventually I was able to change the subject—but not before my confidence had been shaken and my treasured memories tinged.

Right Man remained next to me until a flight attendant asked him to return to his assigned seat for landing. By this time I was more than ready to be alone. It had been a long flight—and in the end, a tiresome conversation.

Right was rather intrusive, when I thought about it—like the way he'd been trying to record the girls' voices against their will, invading their space.

And recording me, even as I protested.

It was at that point that I discovered that my precious photographs were gone, which was even more disconcerting than his penetrating demeanor.

The searing LA sun couldn't begin to penetrate the confusion I felt as I made my way to immigration. I lagged behind as I continued opening and closing different pockets of my purse and carry-on, searching almost frantically for my pictures.

Suddenly I felt a tap on my shoulders. Right Man had once again materialized beside me.

"Where did *you* come from?" I made no attempt to keep the annoyance from my voice.

Right Man leaned into my shoulder as though he were trying to imitate the picture he had found so objectionable. "I waited for you," he intoned, trying unsuccessfully to interject an aura of mystery. "I wanted to see you one more time," he added in an insinuating whisper.

I walked faster, but the infuriating man kept pace with me. I wanted to get away to about the same degree I wanted to stop and ask about the photos.

Could he have accidentally picked them up along with his belongings? I knew he hadn't.

In the end I didn't say a word. When we reached the point where American citizens head one way and foreigners the other, Right Man disappeared into the crowd.

I didn't realize it then, but in that instant my enchanted Japanese summer was over. My season of affliction was about to begin.

CHAPTER 2

A Blinding Sun

And you may find yourself living in a shotgun shack
And you may find yourself in another part of the world
And you may find yourself behind the wheel of a large automobile
And you may find yourself in a beautiful house, with a beautiful wife
And you may ask yourself, well…how did I get here?

TALKING HEADS, "ONCE IN A LIFETIME," 1981

Some religions contend that we exist in a spiritual form before we are born; others attest that we are reborn over and over again, living multiple lives. I had no firm beliefs one way or another. All I knew was that in Japan I had found myself feeling comfortable with ways that were foreign to my upbringing. Perhaps it was just that inside me there was some void I was trying to fill, and that I was latching on to Japan as my remedy.

ON A MAY EVENING IN rural Michigan years earlier, in 1969, the slow-setting sun was beckoning me outside. Straining to catch a glimpse out the living room picture window from my seat at the dinner table, I noticed the tops of trees waving in the warm spring breeze, beckoning me outdoors to play some more. Even on the harshest of winter days, I wasn't one to stay inside.

I had been playing since my return from kindergarten at around noon, but as usual it hadn't been enough. Forcing down what remained of the powdered milk concoction in my cup, I jumped up, dropped off my dishes at the sink, and headed toward the back door. My parents were still eating when I made my exit—Walter Cronkite and my baby sister together held their attention.

It seemed like a particularly fine evening for a bike ride—sunny and warm. Despite my young age, I was allowed to pedal down the road for several hundred feet, as long as I stopped for the occasional car that might happen along (my neighborhood offered no sidewalks). And so, with the intent of making my way to the ends of my little earth, I mounted my bike and prepared for takeoff.

I peddled as vigorously as my five-year-old legs could allow—all the while hugging the weed-fringed edge of our gravel road. My trusty training wheels held me upright as the red, white, and blue tassels that dangled from my handlebars danced like hula girls. I squinted at the bright light of the low-setting sun.

Several miles further down the road, my grandmother, who lived a few country miles away, was returning from her factory job in the city. In the garish sunshine she was having trouble seeing brake lights in front of her, and it crossed her mind that the unusual brightness from that big, red, blinding sun might cause an accident somewhere.

Just as I was approaching the invisible boundary my parents had set for me, my ears detected the ominous rumbling of an old car. Instantly stopping and lowering my feet to the ground, I glanced over my shoulder to observe an advancing ball of billowing dust, from the center of which gleamed a smiling chrome bumper.

Moments later I was in the air—worried, as I still vividly recall, that I would fall onto the huge prickly bush several feet below me. Across the road under the oak tree, I could see my father cradling a small girl. He yelled back over his shoulder to my mother, who was standing on the stoop: "Call Barker's ambulance!"

Then, within a split second, my chest began to heave. My vantage point changed, and I was staring up at my father, regretting that I just vomited all over his work shirt.

"The Accident" quite nearly killed me, but before school started again in the fall, I was back on a new bicycle, bravely churning my little legs to propel myself up and down the road, even waving to the poor neighbor who inadvertently hit me. Despite my face having been smashed to smithereens and losing my left eye, I was resilient.

In my grade school years, I wouldn't have thought twice about my injuries, had it not been for the other kids at school. It seemed as though they were always whispering. Real or imagined, the first letter of any hushed conversation coincided with the first letter of my name. The same kids who had sent me get well cards during the summer were all too quick to make fun of the scars and facial deformities I now sported. My cat-eye glasses *(the left-side lens of which was always dirty because I didn't know enough to clean it)* and I weren't exactly popular. I took solace in being outside, either in our yard or on my grandparents' farm.

But as I progressed to junior and then senior high, my private adventures no longer compensated for the lack of acceptance of which I was so poignantly aware. In my social misery, I became argumentative and at the same time withdrawn—a real handful for my distressed mother. I was so difficult that there were times she would threaten to send me away, to consign me to foster care for my mouthy insolence. During those years all I could think about from my side was vacating my cramped corner of the world. I wanted to go someplace where people would look beyond my scars and my sagging bad eye, or better yet, just plain not see them. I knew I was headed for trouble of some kind.

I would have continued down this path had it not been for the arrival in the daily mail of an intriguing flyer advertising a summer exchange program involving students from Japan. Our family, like many living in farm country, was involved with 4-H, and our county extension service was looking for volunteers to participate. On a "why not?" whim my mother sent in our application. This was the start of something big—a new sun was about to rise.

At the time we received the flyer, I knew nothing of Japan beyond the smattering of facts I had gleaned from history and social studies classes. National and world events seemed so far away and uncontrollable that my family rarely talked about them. Our insular experience of life was being played out in a simple place where family gatherings were written up in a weekly column for the village newspaper. People gadded about, and that's how we learned of happenings—the ones that mattered, anyway.

I did wonder about Japan though, after receiving that flyer—how its people were doing after their devastating defeat. Had they been able to repair all that damage? Were they still angry with Americans? Was it still a country filled with pagodas, geisha girls, and chunky sumo wrestlers? With the prospect of an international visitor venturing into our neck of the woods, I was curious. Whenever I heard "Japan" or "Japanese" on the evening news, I perked up and remained keenly attuned.

Japan was definitely on the American radar in 1979. In a little more than three decades after WWII had ended, the big red sun had again risen, this time assaulting our shores with miniature Toyota and Datsun cars. The evening news was filled with stories about our big three automakers being under siege, a topic of particular concern to Michiganders like ourselves. Many automotive workers, my father included, had struggled with unemployment in the mid-seventies. There were protests in Detroit. Proud UAW men took out their frustrations by smashing defenseless and unoffending Toyotas with baseball bats.

My father was too locally focused to devote much thought to matters beyond our county line road, beyond his control, so he never really said much about the whole import situation. Even so, one afternoon my curiosity got the better of me, and I approached my mild-mannered dad with a question: Did he blame the Japanese for what was happening to our economy? Putting down his Sunday paper long enough to glance over at me for effect, he offhandedly replied, "Those little shits and their cheap cars." He followed this up with a couple of comments that seemed to pin our economic woes on our own less-than-patriotic consumers. He couldn't fathom why red-blooded Americans would buy an import car over one manufactured by their neighbors. A video-cassette recorder, sure, but a car? "Buy American for Christ's sake!"

That was the extent of our serious talk regarding Japan. My family generally left politics and religion off the table, opting instead to deal with life on a day-to-day, person-to-person basis. Every individual deserved a chance, especially the *real*—translate "in person"—Japanese exchange student who was about to enter our home.

After our exchange of introductory letters, Yuki Higashi, my mail-order friend, arrived at our home wearing preppy, clean-cut clothes and long, silky black hair pulled back into a smooth ponytail. She was petite and refined, the polar opposite of myself. Her answers to my chatty, often rapid-fire questions were always efficient: "Yes," "No," and "Oh, I don't know" were common responses. Reserved as she was in all regards, I chalked up Yuki's quiet nature to her culture. From all reports Japanese women were followers—lagging behind men—so I didn't take Yuki's lack of conversational fortitude too personally. It was my job to warm her up, to Americanize her.

I spent the next few days gingerly trying to get to know the girl. I tried to talk a bit less and observe a little more. She had brought us all gifts, various traditional things—summer kimonos, fancy snacks, and knickknacks. These items, along with her roller ball stick of "sock glue" (*something she used to keep her knee highs in perfect position*) and fancy pink eye drops, were infinitely interesting and became the type of topical fodder I used to reach Yuki's soul.

Over the next few weeks, we shared good times and laughs—but I couldn't get a read on what she thought of me or my family. Yuki was so sophisticated that I could only imagine her opinion of our rather loose lot. Over time I came to expect that I would crack the nut that was Yuki Higashi, but I never did figure out what was going on behind her inscrutable dark eyes.

Despite Yuki's cool nature, by the end of the summer my Japanese "sister" and I had formed a bond of sorts. Neither of us would say we were "close," but I assessed us to be at least decent friends and was pretty sure Yuki felt the same. All I know is that when Yuki left I lost it. I mourned her departure as though my most intimate friend had fallen off the planet. And in those days, having a friend half a world away, with only lagging airmail by which to communicate was pretty much like having a pal on the moon.

The fall after Yuki left, I was back in school for my junior year, doing what I had always done—evading the boys who called me "dead eye." And I would have continued in this manner, with no nobler goal other than to avoid being picked on, had it not been for an amazing turn of events. Two months after Yuki left Michigan, she invited me to participate in the second leg of the exchange—to spend the following summer at her family home in Tokyo! This was how the exchange program was supposed to work, but Yuki had originally evaded the issue by making clear that she could not host a visit, even during the summer, due to the importance of her studies.

Quite unexpectedly my new best friend had come through, and my parents, thinking the trip might turn me around, were supportive of my going, as long as I kept my act together during the school year leading up to the event. This was tough because I was hell-bent on escaping my circumstances, which to my way of thinking necessitated lying and generally sneaking around. As it turned out, it was only by the skin of my teeth that I was permitted to board the plane.

It was early in July 1980 when I got my first look at Japan, and I was amazed.

Taking a tour bus into the heart of Tokyo, I thought I'd been fooled by my informational resources. The out-of-date library books I'd borrowed from school still made Japan look a bit backward. Where were all the kimonos and rickshaws? From what I could see, Japan was completely modern.

After I had spent the night in a dormitory (I was awed to learn that it was part of the 1964 Olympic village!), my best friend in the whole wide world arrived to spring me from the exchange group and escort me to her home somewhere on the outskirts of the big city. I say "big city," but it all seemed quite compact. As soon as I hit the streets, I was taken aback by the size disparity between everything around me and my accustomed reality. Although I tried to follow Yuki's queue and glide smoothly through the throngs of pedestrians, the spaces invisibly allotted to living and moving had simply not been designed for someone of my stature.

Several train stations, a dozen flights of stairs, and a long and narrow winding street later we finally reached the Higashi house, where Yuki slid open a set of glass doors and called out to someone. In response a diminutive old lady with jet-black hair materialized to greet us. It was Yuki's grandmother, who instantly and with surprising fluidity fell to her knees when she caught sight of me.

"Irrashaimase" ("Welcome"), she said, as she proceeded to fold her body in half, her forehead to my amazement nearly touching the floor.

I returned with the formal return greeting I had learned from language tapes.

Yuki's grandmother, bowing again, uttered something I could not understand, and I dutifully returned the gesture.

Introductions complete, Yuki proceeded to unsnap her sandal straps, after which, with her footwear still on, she turned to face the front door we had just entered and gracefully stepped up backward onto a wooden ledge, shucking her shoes in the process.

Despite my best efforts to gracefully follow my sister's lead, my old-fashioned buckles wouldn't cooperate, and I ended up standing barefoot on the tile floor.

"Ah…you are not supposed to step there," Yuki chided as she opened a cupboard, pulled out a white towel, and handed it to me. "Here, you can wipe your feet with this."

I was taken aback by the protocol. Hadn't Yuki noticed that I had gone barefooted most of the previous summer back home? Was she aware that I often went to bed without washing my feet?

Yuki instructed me to lift my suitcase so she could wipe the wheels and then to follow her up a set of steep stairs. A good portion of my big feet hung off the narrow treads.

At the top of the stairs was a narrow hallway, lined with windows on the right and paper doors on the left. Yuki parted the middle set of sliding panels.

"You can use this room," she informed me. "My sister Mari is using a room by the kitchen."

Given the doll-like proportions of the house, I could not imagine where Mari would sleep, and I felt bad for displacing her.

Observing my puzzled reaction, Yuki assured me, "My parents bought her a stereo, so she's fine."

Inside Mari's room was a second set of screens, which Yuki opened to reveal a compact space. Our rooms were connected much like those in a hotel suite.

After unpacking my things, Yuki showed me the rest of the house. Besides the three bedrooms upstairs, there was a toilet room divided in two by the urinal section and the "all purpose" floor commode; a bathing/laundry room with a shower area and short, deep tub; a kitchen with pantry; and a living/dining space that doubled at night as the grandparents' sleeping area. It was an extremely utilitarian house, complete with a small, orderly garden.

Yuki's mom, or *okaasan*, was in the kitchen cooking a special welcome dinner, and Yuki went in to help her. I sat down with her grandparents at a low table in the TV room. They were watching what appeared to be a variety show. On the screen a teenage girl in a frilly smock was singing her heart out as the studio audience clapped to the beat. A theatrical performance par excellence, her facial expressions were coy and her movements clearly choreographed.

Once the song was over, the host, pulling his microphone cord behind him, went over to the girl and appeared to conduct an interview. Whenever the singer answered a question, the teenaged audience would exclaim "*eeeeee-hhhhhh!*" in a rising tone of surprise, in response to which the performer would cover her mouth with her fingertips and giggle.

In the corner of the room, a fan oscillated from side to side, its swath alternately providing relief from the late afternoon heat to Yuki's *ojiisan* and *obaasan*. The fan was nicer than any I'd seen back home, streamlined, with fancy push-button controls. Observing me staring at the fan, Yuki's grandmother got up and made some adjustment before disappearing into the kitchen. She returned with a cold towel, Yuki in tow. Before me Yuki placed a small plate of wrapped treats and a soda can labeled Calpis, which sounded a lot like "cow piss" when she said it. Strange name aside, the milky white drink was sweet and cool.

"Do you like this show?" Yuki asked me.

A group of three boys had taken the stage, and they too seemed to be acting. I responded politely that the program was "interesting" (*in a Donny and Marie kind of way*) and asked her in return what she thought of it.

"It's not my type," Yuki replied evasively. "But Mari and my grandparents enjoy it."

Several hours later Yuki's father, *otoosan*, arrived home from his factory manager job, and the four of us—Yuki, her parents, and I—sat down around the small Western table in the kitchen. The grandparents ate at the same low table in the TV room at which they had been seated ever since my arrival and Mari dined alone in her makeshift pantry/bedroom.

The conversation didn't exactly flow, but Yuki's dad understood some English from working abroad, and Yuki, of course, was able to fill in the blanks. My dining companions were amused when I asked for butter to put on my rice and added a dash of soy sauce to enhance the flavor. Apparently rice was to be eaten plain.

I was forewarned that I would be on my own most weekdays, and, sure enough, the next morning Yuki and Mari departed early to attend summer cram school. That first day I remained close to the house, but as I became familiar with my surroundings I began more and more to venture out. Each morning, before the midday sun got the better of me, I'd stroll as far as I could in one direction or the other and try to find my way back—which I always did, a surprising feat, given the seemingly nonsensical layout of the streets and alleys.

Along the way I'd stop in quaint shops that carried an amazing variety for their size. There was a *panya*, or bread shop, with fancy rolls baked in the shapes of cartoon characters, as well as a *senbeiya* that featured my new favorite snack, rice crackers. Each purchase, no matter how small, was gift wrapped in a fancy angular fashion, as though I'd spent much more.

The mom & pop shops were anchored by a department store situated next to the train station that carried an array of character goods, the likes of which I'd never before seen. While Americans were stuck on Looney Tunes and Mickey Mouse metal lunch boxes, Japan had all sorts of cute household and fashion items with kitties and bunnies on them. And the electronics? They were beyond belief in function and appearance. If we had half a dozen stereos in our local Sears & Roebuck back home, the Japanese had two or three times as many, available in several pastel shades.

Just as I found the places and people infinitely fascinating, the Japanese were openly curious about me. Sometimes they reacted in surprise to my height and commented that I was "big"—but mostly folks simply stared and whispered. This attention was far different from the taunts I had received at school. It was as though I were a celebrity of sorts, someone people wanted to talk to but were afraid to disturb. I actually enjoyed being the object of this type of attention.

On some days Yuki, fearing I might be lonely and bored, would ask classmates to escort me around. We would meet up at the local train station, and they would lead me into the heart of the city, where I'd be shown this or that shopping district or historical place. Gradually Yuki's friends became mine—providing me with companionship I'd lacked back home.

Every day was an adventure, though along the way I suffered a few mishaps. It took me a couple of weeks, for example, to choreograph a fluid duck—or dip, rather, as was the way of the graceful Japanese—at just the right point to avoid hitting my head on doorways. Worse than this, in the beginning I had unwittingly used the Japanese floor commode backward, causing mini disasters that took me a half roll of toilet paper to rectify. Eventually, by trial and error, I pinpointed my mistake. The toilet was shaped like a urinal set horizontally into the floor. The technique was to squat over it, facing the hemispherical hood, which apparently was intended to act as a backsplash.

I was just getting my Japanese groove on—learning new routines and making friends, when I was told I would have to leave. Per the requirements of the exchange program, I was scheduled to attend a camp with other exchange participants across the region. According to Yuki most of the Americans would be attending along with their Japanese counterparts, but she had been granted an exception for her studies, and I'd be obliged to go alone.

Feeling a bit guilty about sending me off to the countryside, Yuki was extra attentive in helping me pack. She ensured that I would have in my possession plenty of snacks, basic medical supplies, an umbrella, and even a rain poncho. When I asked about the rain gear, Yuki informed me that the place I was going to was still in *tsuyuu*—the rainy season. At that point, mesmerized, I watched her take a few tissues and mold them into a tiny, ghostlike shape. Around the neck of the ghost she tied a string.

"This," she informed me, "is for good weather."

"A ghost?" I asked.

Yuki laughed. "No it's a Buddhist monk."

With this she hung the little monk ghost above her window with a pushpin. "It's praying that the sun shines for you at Kurohime Camp."

"Rain, rain, go away," I thought a little ruefully. Once when I was little I had wished upon a star for a particular doll, and though I'd received it in the very same week, I knew my prayer had been no miracle—it was just my incessant hinting and my mother finally relenting. What would a little wad of Kleenex do? All I knew is that I wanted the next few days to fly by, rain or no rain.

CHAPTER 3

Moon Rabbits

I had been in Japan for only a short while, and already I was falling hard. My impressions from before the trip had been entirely off the mark. The Japanese were hardly lagging behind; in many ways they were far advanced. Traditions, protocol, and prayer provided in my mind a beautiful backdrop and structure, fostering ample opportunity for imaginative flights. Someday the tissue monk would be a commodity sold in every color, depending on one's particular weather wish—I could just see it.

I ARRIVED AT MY CAMP destination after a long train trek followed by an unnerving bus ride. Nauseous from the winding foothill roads, I stumbled off the bus and woozily toddled toward a woman holding a clipboard. She found my name on her list and pointed me toward a sign labeled "Himalaya."

As I took my place and awaited further instruction, I noticed that my fellow campers were much younger than I had anticipated. Shouldering backpacks large enough to tip them over, most appeared to be in elementary school. Finally two guys of about my age appeared, one apparently American and the other Japanese. Anxious to salvage my few days away from Tokyo, I quickly went over and introduced myself.

Steve was from California, and he was cute. His friend, Yasu, a tall boy whose hair was accented in orange, was all smiles. When I told them I had been sent alone, they kindly agreed to adopt me and expand their duo into a trio. What had started out to be a lonely trip was showing signs of promise.

As our group was scuttled from activity to activity, Steve and I were swarmed by children who wanted our attention. (As it turned out this was a culture camp for younger kids to learn about Western countries—primarily the United States. Yuki had been a member of this club since she was in grade school, but only the older members travel and host.) We were curiosities, aliens who were expected to make ourselves available to all manner of poking and prodding. Less popular on account of his all-too-common nationality, Yasu stood back and watched in mock amusement as Steve and I dealt with the onslaught. In response to his teasing, I took to making faces.

By the time we were called in to our lodge for dinner, Yasu and I had begun to engage in some horsing around—pushing and nudging each other as we walked. The boy had a good sense of humor, and we had quickly established a connection. Although Steve and I had spent the better part of the afternoon in close proximity due to our mutual diplomatic assignments, it was his silly friend Yasu who captured my attention. And this situation continued through dinner and beyond, until Steve and I were instructed to retire to the segregated American lodges.

The next morning, like a child wanting to get out early and play, I wasted no time making my way back to Himalaya lodge. There I found Yasu, apparently also an early riser, sitting at the kitchen table surrounded by children. He was casually smoking a cigarette and drinking coffee.

Yasu watched me enter the room, and we acknowledged each other with slight nods as he continued to offer himself up for the children's amusement. Contrary to images portrayed in Marlboro commercials, I had never thought of smoking as attractive, but Yasu exuded a certain swagger in conjunction with his habit that made it seem cool.

After breakfast everyone gathered in the large tatami room where we were to receive instructions for the day. As Yasu silently took a seat behind me, the not altogether unwelcome tension I had felt the evening before returned.

Unable to understand most of what was being announced by the camp leader, I let my mind wander, envisioning how the day might go—more specifically, how the interaction between Yasu and myself might progress.

As I daydreamed I thought I felt something swipe across my back. I sat still with my thoughts, though wondering what could have caused this odd sensation. Then I felt it again. Slowly and methodically Yasu was writing something with his finger across my back. By the letter *E* I got the message. He was blatantly conveying his love. In that instant I wanted to fall backward into his arms, but with everyone around I could only turn around and smile.

All day we teased each other with sidelong glances and intentional contact—brushes against each other that precipitated in me an intense hormonal rush. What we were going to do with such feelings I had no clue, but somehow we needed to find an outlet. Finally that evening, as the campers lined up to trek to a campfire party in the woods, we looked at each other, both recognizing that this might be our opportunity. Yasu glanced meaningfully upward toward the second-floor stairs before looking at me and nodding. After he had repeated the series of gestures, I caught on to the signal and nodded in affirmation. Wordlessly, our plan had been hatched.

As the line moved forward and campers exited into the starry night, Yasu and I separately retreated to the dark cabin loft, where we hid in separate futon closets, waiting until the coast was clear. Yasu exited first and called for me to join him.

Wasting no time, he draped his arms around my waist and squeezed tightly, after which he held me at arm's length, took in a deep breath, and leaned forward.

Ours was the most perfectly synchronized kiss. It was straight out of a movie scene; not one moment felt awkward, and we made out as though there would be no tomorrow. After several minutes of pure passion we took a break and lay companionably side by side. There in the darkness we giggled and sighed, our mixed reactions the result of our knowledge that what we were doing couldn't possibly last.

The only source of light came from a sliver of moonlight streaming in through a single window. As I gazed toward it, Yasu suddenly sat up, turned toward me and put his hands around my face.

After staring a few moments, he announced, "You are so pretty, cutie, and lovely."

These English words sounded more foreign to me than the Japanese conversations that had by this time surrounded me for weeks. Not one boy back home had ever complimented me on my looks. In fact, I couldn't recall *anyone* ever having used words like "cute" or "pretty" in reference to me.

Still, Yasu's kind confession made me uncomfortable.

"I'm not," I countered, looking down. I told Yasu he was crazy for saying I was pretty, but he insisted it was true.

After examining my features for a minute or two, Yasu reached behind his head and wordlessly produced a chain—a necklace of some kind that he promptly fastened around my neck.

As the chain dangled against my chest, I felt a warm, melting sensation glide over me like a wave. Then, like a romantic lead, Yasu rose and pulled me to a standing position. He led me to the window, where he looked out and upward.

"Can you see the rabbits?" he asked.

I was taken aback, uncertain of what Yasu was talking about. It was dark, and rabbits—including Japanese ones, to the best of my knowledge—didn't fly.

Yasu began to sing, and the only words I could make out were "rabbit" and "moon." He tried to teach me the first line.

I couldn't understand why Yasu would associate rabbits with the moon, but from what I had come to know about Japanese people, there had to be a good reason behind the inferred connection. As I was to learn later, this folklore corresponds to Westerners looking at the moon and visualizing Swiss cheese. Yasu simply lacked the English facility to explain it.

We had been alone for only twenty minutes or so when Yasu announced that we should go outside and join the others; he insisted we would be missed and that a search would ensue. The boy who thought I was pretty could have had anything he wanted at that moment, but he chose to be responsible and keep us out of trouble.

The next day the tissue monk Yuki had made failed in his mission; it rained nonstop. Even so, although sharing an umbrella was awkward, Yasu and I were inseparable. During that time I tried to capture his essence, every bit of his spirit, knowing that a good-bye was inevitable.

On the last day, as the flat-faced tour busses arrived to take everyone back to wherever it was they had come from, Yasu and I felt as close as conjoined twins as we waited to board our respective rides. My assigned bus to the train station was already nearly full. Yasu and Steve were to return to Kanagawa—the area just west of Tokyo—and would be taking a different ride, scheduled to depart shortly thereafter.

As we hemmed and hawed, avoiding the inevitable leave-taking, a chorus of shrill cries rose from the forest that surrounded the camp.

"What's that noise?" I asked Yasu, startled. I'd heard it before in Tokyo but had forgotten to ask Yuki about it.

Yasu didn't seem to know what I was talking about, so I tried to imitate the piercing sound. When he heard my rendition, he chortled.

"Oh, you mean the *mi mi mi* and the *kana kana kana*?" he asked.

I affirmed, and Yasu explained that it was *semi*.

I had no idea what a semi was—at least not in this context—but Yasu informed me it was a kind of insect.

"He is crying for love," he explained with a hint of the dramatic. "He was in the ground for many years, but now he is free and wants girlfriend."

I had no idea what the bug looked like but was convinced I had heard similar cries in Michigan. In Japan the semi were so loud they simply couldn't be ignored.

Yasu proceeded to tell me the saddest love story—about how semi lived above ground for just a few days, only to die after consummation.

As I thought about the lonely creatures, I heard the last call to board my waiting bus.

"I see you again?" Yasu asked rather urgently.

"Yes. Yes," I assured him. "In two years I will see you again in Japan. I promise."

Almost everyone had taken a seat on their assigned busses, with Yasu and I the sole holdouts. Japanese kids and American teens stared out of the windows at us. The connection between us was no secret, and all were waiting to see what we would do.

Tugging at Yasu's orange T-shirt sleeve, I slowly mouthed the words we had repeated to each other so many times within the span of the four-day immersion camp. At this point there was to be no more stalling.

The bus ride was punctuated with squeals of laughter as Japanese and American young people (our bus was filled primarily with teens) tried to communicate. What one person didn't understand another did, and the circuitous conversations went on in this unique way.

Ignoring the chatty commotion, I stared glumly out of the rain-streaked window. The scenery outside was a blur as the bus sped through those winding turns toward the bottom of the hill. It felt to me as though we weren't on a road at all but on some sort of black-and-white spiral that was gyrating into nothingness. How could this have happened? How could I have met the boy of my dreams halfway around the world? It seemed like an impossible situation.

A tear slid unchecked down my left cheek as I thought about what it was I would be going back to. In only a few short weeks, I would return to Michigan, undoubtedly to live out my years on a dirt road to nowhere. I made a bet with myself that a certain drop of drizzle zigzagging down the window glass would make it to the bottom before the lone tear dropped from my chin.

When I arrived back at the Higashi house, I was not in the best mood. I should have been walking on clouds over having met Yasu, but saying goodbye had left a hole in my heart. On top of this, the left side of my face had begun to ache. The wires that had held my bones together after the accident still lay underneath my skin, and they were sensitive to changes in the atmospheric pressure. Feeling terrible all the way around, I remained in my futon bed for two days. On the third day, Yuki entered my room with a letter.

The single-page note written in clean longhand opened with the words, "My Dear Amiable Stacy."

I turned to look questioningly at Yuki. *"Amiable?* I've never heard this word."

Yuki brought a dictionary from her desk, and together we discovered that *amiable* meant "pleasant"—perhaps something like "pretty," a word that didn't seem to fit me.

The letter was written in very broken English, and it took me several passes to get through it. In the meantime Yuki grew uncharacteristically impatient.

"What did he write?" she asked, wide eyed.

Yuki was ordinarily a very private person, so I was a bit surprised by the intensity of her interest. Wanting to understand the letter fully, I handed it to her. As she read I leaned over her shoulder, desperately wanting to know what she thought.

"Well?" I asked. Now I was the impatient one.

"He certainly likes you," she conceded with a smile.

This opinion coming from Yuki added in my own mind to Yasu's credibility. She was much too cool to be less than honest.

The letter ended with a promise. Yasu would come to see me on my last full day in Japan. He knew my travel group would be gathering at a hotel not far from his home, and he could meet Yuki and me there.

The thought of seeing Yasu once more, even though it was only to say good-bye again, was enough to get me out of bed. There was really no time to waste, as the days of my charmed Japanese existence were fast dwindling.

Like the open air and trees that had called me out to play when I was small, the sights, sounds, and smells of the coolest place on earth beckoned me forth to discover and learn. From the city cock crowing at first light to the now familiar sound of music blaring from a public loudspeaker down the street, calling children to their public exercises before breakfast, to the narrow streets with their vendors, to the smell of freshly baked rice crackers and cedar incense burning from family altars, to the first fruits laid out for generations past, to fancy goods everywhere, to the attention I received whenever I stepped past our garden gate, all of this beckoned me.

During my final days, Yuki and her friends escorted me around the city to take in more famous places and do what teenagers around the world do: hang out at fast food places, shopping centers, and parks. And while we were having the best of times, I grieved in advance the inevitable conclusion; the acceptance of my Tokyo friends was something I would sorely miss.

On my last night in Yuki's home, as I was thinking about the friends I would be leaving, Yuki announced that the entire gang was en route to her house. Thoughtfully, they had arranged an impromptu going away party on my behalf.

As we talked and played cards, I jokingly asked whether anyone would be willing to hide me away so I wouldn't have to return. But the grand scheme I humorously envisioned was entirely impossible. During the final toast to my safe travels and future, several of my new friends promised to make the trip out to the airport to see me off.

The next day I found Yasu sitting in the hotel lobby, as promised, waiting for me. Soundlessly I walked up from behind and tapped him on the shoulder, at which he instantly jumped to his feet. Smiling, he introduced himself to Yuki. Protocol complete, we decided to find a quieter location for our good-byes. The evening was booked with a "farewell Japan" dinner and other group activities, and I had just an hour of free time. We slipped upstairs to my assigned room, with Yuki in tow.

Once in the room, Yuki tried to make conversation with Yasu in English so I would be included, but Yuki's language skills were so advanced that my poor boyfriend reverted to Japanese. Intimidated, or perhaps just a little embarrassed, Yasu got up to smoke.

Sticking a cigarette in his mouth, he mumbled a rhetorical "May I?" as he walked over to the window.

Instantly devising a joke, I jumped up and snatched Yasu's lighter as he pulled it from his pocket.

Yasu laughed. This was the way the two of us had been at camp: mischievous and playful. He protested, "No. I need!"

A mini struggle ensued, but my arm was longer than Yasu's, and I let the lighter fall through the open window, looking at Yuki and winking. Thankfully, she caught on and offered to retrieve it.

As she walked to the door she called back, "I'll be back in fifteen minutes or so." Of course it wouldn't take Yuki that long to walk down several flights and back up, but my sister was smart enough to know that my boyfriend and I needed privacy.

Yasu lost no time in seizing the opportunity. Grabbing my hand, he pulled me down with him toward the bed. But instead of spending tender moments kissing, as we had done in the lodge, he began to aggressively pull at my clothes. He seemed determined to have more, more than I could or would give. This time I would be the one to call timeout.

"No, Yasu. I want, but I can't," I told him. I couldn't begin to imagine informing my parents I'd gotten knocked up while in Japan.

Yasu took a deep breath and sat up. Laughing good-naturedly, he retorted, "Now I need smoke, but no light!"

Holding hands, we cuddled until Yuki returned, and then the three of us slowly made our way back to the lobby, where we would say good-bye yet again.

Standing at the hotel lobby door, Yasu reached deep into the pockets of his white painter pants and pulled out a handful of change. He dumped the coins into my cupped hands, instructing me to call before I went to bed.

After dinner I put every last coin into one of the lobby payphones. Sigh after sigh, "I love you" after "forever" and "never forget," we talked as the timer on the phone ticked down. Through the warning beep until the dial tone took over, we expressed our undying love.

In a daze I headed back to my room. I had a secret stash that would help numb my pain—sample bottles of whiskey I had picked up on my way to the hotel. I was particularly thankful at that moment that I had been able to purchase liquor in Japan without an ID check. Several whiskey samplers later I lay in a stupor on the bed.

Thoughts of Yasu played themselves out over and over again in my mind. Rolling over onto my side, I gripped my pillow tightly. As I drifted off, I could almost feel the weight of Yasu against me. It was then that I devised a plan to believe at all times that he was with me. I would make my own reality by reproducing the touch, smells, and image of Yasu in my mind. I would take Japan and Yasu back to America with me.

The next day, to my surprise, many of Yuki's friends actually did come to see me off at Narita Airport, a considerable distance from town by train. Each brought some trinket for me to remember them by. Among the gifts was a wrapped box. I wanted to open it in front of everyone, but my travel group was already down the escalator. I had to say my final farewell and catch up.

Taking a seat near my departure gate, I realized that the cultural ambience around me was diminishing. It felt as though meaning and purpose were being sucked out of the air and that the little that was left made breathing difficult. Souvenirs, my memories, and the occasional correspondence were all I would have to sustain me over the next couple of years. It was then that I remembered: I still had one more memento to discover—one last gift to unwrap.

Of all the trinkets I had received that day, this one was probably the most expensive—and, at first glance, the most mundane: a nice, but rather common looking pen. It turned out, however, that the pen was not as it appeared. Inside its silver shaft was a secret I would find myself unable to understand.

Having no clue to how to explain the instrument, I glanced around, hoping for someone nearby to help. Among the tourists and business travelers, I spotted a younger Japanese man. Perhaps he could reveal the mystery and give me one last dose of that coveted culture before I made my final departure.

CHAPTER 4

My One-Eyed Talisman

I had inhaled Japan and in the process experienced an intoxicating high. The summer before I had been intrigued by Yuki and her ways, but now, having been exposed to some of the underpinnings that defined her subtle style, I was desperate for more. My memories of the short visit wouldn't sustain me. I needed a culture dealer—a direct source of connection.

BEFORE ENTERING MY ROOM IN Michigan for the first time in six weeks, I stopped short. The lush green shag carpet appeared to crawl. On the surface it appeared clean, but I knew it was not. Having experienced what it was like to live in a house where outside dirt was left behind in the entryway, I longed for the simple mats—the tatami that covered the floors of Yuki's home.

Not knowing how to proceed when everything that mattered seemed to have been lost to me, I fell back onto my bed and stared morosely up at the ceiling. Lying there in deep contemplation over my new reality—a reality that extended far beyond our county lines—I could feel a broken mattress spring poking my back. I had slept on the same mattress since I was a toddler. Suddenly it had become incredibly uncomfortable.

Turning onto my side, I surveyed the contents of my room. As I lay there, a sick feeling washed over me. There was dull insignificance in everything around me. Instead of being overwhelmed by an abundance of culture, I was taken aback by its void.

My desktop arrangement, if one could call it that, consisted of a cowbell, a hairy and nondescript creature I had won at a carnival game, and a Hollie Hobbie–like doll, all of it relegated in my estimation to meaningless "crap" at this point. My dresser too was adorned with knickknacks that had been sitting in the same location for years. It was time for a change.

I was beyond tired, but the condition of my room made it impossible for me to rest. It no longer reflected my style, and I couldn't feel sufficiently at home even to drift off into sleep. Inspired by a felt need to change up my surroundings, I rose and cleared everything from the top of my dresser. Inside my suitcase I had the makings of an altar.

For my dresser centerpiece, I chose the scrapbook I had assembled over the summer. Inside it were ticket stubs, pamphlets, and various photos—a nearly complete reflection of my trip, with the exception of some important pictures that had come up missing on my return flight. Off to one side, I placed a small set of black lacquered drawers; on the other, a Japanese teacup and two folding fans—my small, feminine one and the larger autographed version I'd received from Right Man on the plane.

In front of everything else, I positioned a daruma doll. Why they called it a doll I'm still not sure; it looked more like a red ball with a painted face. I had purchased the three-inch papier-mâché roly-poly, the smallest among several available versions, for a paltry 300 yen from a temple near Yuki's house. Apparently it was a Buddhist talisman capable of granting one wish.

My Japanese sister had told me about the magical powers of the daruma. It was surprising to me that a smart girl like Yuki would go along with superstitions like the tissue monk and the daruma, but I had observed her many times throwing smoke over her shoulder at the temples and suspected that she prayed in earnest. To invoke the daruma's powers, I took a black marker from my desk and drew one dot in the white of his right eye. He would not receive his second pupil until I saw Yasu's face again.

In my lonely, anxious state it would have been comforting to burn some calming cedar incense, but I had none. So I left my prayers with my little round god, took a seat at my childhood desk, and proceeded to write out a postcard to each of my new friends, along with a letter to Yasu. Ten personalized notes later I was finished. Then, as I was about to put away my pen, I remembered that there was one more message I needed to compose.

"*It was nice talking to you on the plane,*" I began. "*If you happen to find my pictures among your things, could you return them to me? They are sadly missing.*"

After wishing the Sado guy good luck with his studies, I closed with "If you want to enjoy a real American holiday, you should visit Michigan during your Christmas break." He was down in Louisiana, so I was pretty sure the invitation was a stretch. It was unlikely he would take me up on it, so I made the offer without even asking permission.

As I started my senior year, The Vapors, a British punk group I'd never heard of before, had me pegged. Their quirky song titled "I'm Turning Japanese" hit our local airwaves just after my return, and I felt it was a sign. On top of this, *Shogun* was the hottest show that fall, and I was actually able to understand a good portion of the Japanese, which generally was not subtitled. The world really was turning in the direction of the Rising Sun in new ways, and I was highly attuned to this fact.

I felt special in my newfound knowledge of the world and compartmentalized a great deal. Separating myself from family and classmates, I tried to create my own miniature Japanese world. Airmail letters were my one and only tie, and the highlight of each day was the half-mile walk from my bus stop to our mailbox. During school I'd visualize our mailman's dusty blue suburban stopping in front of our house and him placing a red-white-and-blue-fringed airmail envelope in the box. Every third day or so my reward was waiting.

The letters were almost entirely from Yasu, with an occasional note from Yuki mixed in. Yasu's letters were dreamy and rambling, and I read each of them multiple times in an effort to capture exactly what he was trying to convey with his limited English. I pulled hard to siphon every nuance from his words.

Yuki was invariably busy with school, so her notes were short. She expressed that her classmates, my new friends, were equally busy and that it was too time consuming for them to write me in English, so I shouldn't expect much from them in the way of correspondence. She indicated, though, that they all thought of me and had told her to say hi. This I found hard to take, because they all meant so much to me, but at least I had my boyfriend and my best friend to sustain me.

One day, next to an envelope with Yasu's familiar scrawl, I found a small padded package from Louisiana. When I saw it I thought to myself, *"Well, if I only have two or three Japanese friends I can count on, perhaps I should pay a bit more attention to this guy; he's one more connection."*

Inside the soft package, I found the "better gifts" Right Man had promised to send when he'd recorded my voice on the plane. There was a small stone Buddha, about five inches tall, and a dragonfly pin made of bamboo. In addition there were two numbered envelopes labeled "I" and "II."

Envelope "I" contained a picture of Right Man dressed in white martial arts garb, a detailed explanation of the gifts and their connection to Sado Island, and a request for a photo. Right Man asked for a "natural image" so he could "feel the same sensation" as if I were standing in the room with him.

"Sensation? What in the heck is he talking about?" I asked myself aloud.

The perceived insinuation struck me as creepy, but the man's English was less than perfect. He most likely failed to understand the subtleties of his word choice.

Package II contained a response to my casual invitation to visit Michigan. He wanted to take me up on the Christmas holiday invitation but expressed concern that my family would be opposed to a Buddhist being in the house during a religious festival. *There was no mention of my missing photo inquiry.*

Overall, the package, completely overdone, reinforced the ambivalent feelings I had about the man. A good part of me wanted to rescind the invitation and conveniently tell him my parents had objected to his visit, but a smaller part of me—the part that wanted to know more about "The Real Japan"—wanted him to come. I would likely be bored silly during the holidays, and he would at least function as a firsthand source for something I craved.

To stem any inappropriate thoughts Right may have been entertaining in my regard, I replied in a "just friends" sort of way, hoping he would understand but still consider the trip. When no response came, I thought it just as well. Frankly, if he had other intentions it was best he didn't come. I wanted a teacher, not a complication.

While Louisiana had fallen silent, letters from Yasu arrived with increasing frequency. My love's expressions improved greatly as he described his feelings for me in ever-increasing detail—placing the two of us together in imaginary scenes engaging in this or that activity. Many times these envisioned scenes were sexual in nature—highly intoxicating doses that incited in me a sense of euphoria mixed with despair.

Although English may have been a challenge for Yasu, his imagination was far more prolific than mine. Just when I thought I'd received the most lustful letter possible. a more potent note would arrive. I was beginning to think Yasu was going a bit too far with the graphic content and to worry about whether, or how, I'd respond in kind, when a letter from Right Man appeared. He had purchased airline tickets for Michigan and was planning to spend most of his winter break at our house. Just like that.

When I carefully informed my parents that a casual invite to a friend had turned into a nearly three-week stay, they were a little miffed. When I added the seemingly extraneous detail that the houseguest would be a twenty-two-year-old man, they were naturally opposed. But because I was by this time relentless in my pursuit of all things Japan, in the end they threw up their hands and reluctantly allowed the planned visit to proceed.

Right Man arrived at Capitol City Airport in mid-December, wearing a plum-colored leisure suit with a beige turtleneck. Upon seeing him again, I instantly felt a sense of regret for having extended the invitation. I recalled the pictures he had likely stolen and our awkward conversation on the plane. At some point, I thought—as soon as conveniently possible—I should make it clear that I was Yasu's girl.

Following the drive home and after showing our guest around, I approached Right as he was unpacking.

"Remember the pictures I showed you on the plane? That guy you said was 'no good' is my boyfriend."

Right said he remembered.

With this I showed Right a fresh picture of Yasu in his school uniform, looking more than respectable, but my guest was unimpressed, commenting offhandedly that the outfit was clearly from a trade school. Then he asked a peculiar question. "He smokes tobacco, doesn't he?"

I wasn't sure what this detail had to do with anything. A lot of young guys smoked. In fact, I ventured to guess that more than 70 percent of Japanese men used tobacco. It seemed a random leap in logic to suggest, as Right implied, that all men who smoked were thereby bad people.

My admission that Yasu did indeed light up upon occasion sent Right into a mini tirade, as he began to rant about smoking, bad boys, stupid people, my lack of knowledge concerning Japan, etc. In the end Right summarized, "You just don't know anything. It's all a game for him."

If I'd already regretted inviting Right when I'd first seen him at the airport, I really rued my decision now. The impetus for the invitation had been my desire to enhance my cultural knowledge, but he was making me feel so stupid, once again shaking the foundation of what I thought I knew so well. Right leaned into my left shoulder.

"You know...I say these things because I don't want you to get hurt."

This intrusion into my personal space reminded me of Right coming up from behind as I made my way from the plane to immigration. Now as then, his presence was entirely too close for comfort.

"That's nice of you," I replied noncommittally, "but I'm done talking to you about my friends."

For better or worse I was stuck with Right for the duration of my winter break, and I'd have to make the best of it.

Over the next few days, I focused on my Japanese studies—the original reason I had asked Right to come. In addition to picking up new words and phrases, Right provided explanations for why things were as they were—both from a Japanese perspective and a scientific mindset—which apparently went hand in hand.

In terms of guidance, Right seemed excessively black and white as he glibly pronounced virtually everything either "good" or "no good." He was never indecisive about his positions; there seemed to be no room for subjectivity. Right exemplified in my mind precisely what one might think of when envisioning a traditional Japanese man—straight out of *Shogun*. Annoying me still further, Right was a chronic "bower"—continuously giving at least a slight nod or bend for arrivals and departures within a room, and he was prone to using Japanese "elegant speech" that emphasized the longer, honorific form of words.

Right liked talking about legends, and his serious nature warmed whenever he spoke of tradition and prewar Japan; he all but ignored the more recent years. In fact, his references to modern culture were limited almost entirely to the West.

Between our tutoring sessions, Right playfully interacted with my family. As fascinated as I was with his country, he seemed to be equally interested in us. It seemed as though every time my younger sister and I turned around, Right was there, camera in hand, telling us we were cute and snapping away. In time, since we avoided the controversial topic of my Tokyo friends, and more specifically of my boyfriend, Right became more relaxed and began to reveal information about himself—fascinating glimpses into his life.

Having endured trauma myself, I was naturally drawn to people with a story—to people who had endured a tragedy or tough circumstance—and I intuited that there was something behind Right's heavy eyes. And so I began to probe. On the plane I had noticed his prominent limp; when I asked about his condition he shared that the injury was the result of a motorcycle accident a year and a half earlier. Prior to the accident, he told me, he had been athletic—enjoying skiing and judo—but now he couldn't participate in any sports.

Right went on to say that shortly after he was injured, while he was recuperating at home, his best friends had gone skiing without him, all perishing in an avalanche. Having had a near-death experience with my own accident, I found that this story gave Right instant credibility in my book. Naturally I found it easier to relate to people who had experienced a tragedy.

Right's presence in the house caused my letters to Yasu to lapse for a few days. Thankfully, on the morning of Christmas Eve I had an opportunity to reconnect—to actually hear my love's voice for the first time in four months.

As one of my Christmas gifts, my parents permitted me to make a ten-minute call to Yasu.

This call was much like the one I had made from the hotel payphone the evening prior to my departure—punctuated by numerous sighs and endless "I love yous." Because I was so nervous, giggling whenever I thought of the intimate details we'd been writing to each other, Yasu took the lead, asking me to close my eyes as he pulled me toward an imaginary bed to lie with him.

After the call I felt a tremendous rush as Yasu's words continued coursing through my veins. I was so hyper I decided I needed to get outside to expend some energy. On a whim I dressed in my one-piece snowmobile suit, stepped outside, and fired up an Arctic Cat sled. Fresh snow had drifted over the fence line that ran from the side of our property back a quarter mile to the woods.

Straddling the seat, I took off standing. I raced back toward the woods, turned around, and skimmed home across the drift tops as fast as I could, aware that if I slowed I'd sink and become buried. More than once in the past I'd experienced becoming stuck far from the house and having to dig and claw my way out of nearly impossible situations unaided. This time I successfully managed to fly across the gaps. Following my run I bounded across the fields in zigzag patterns until my fingers became frozen.

As I parked the snowmobile, I could see through the window that Right Man was up and about. Mr. Chrysanthemum Pond had over the course of the visit become something of an older brother figure to me—looking out for my welfare and general safety in the form of verbal tidbits on the proper way to do this or that. An enduring presence in my life he was evidently not to be, but he did seem to genuinely care. Walking toward the back door, my eyes caught his as he stood in our living room peering out a window. Right nodded to acknowledge my wave.

On December 26 I received letters ninety-three and ninety-four from Yasu. My call to him had taken me back to the camp lodge loft as he spoke lovingly of his desire to hold me once again. His written words, however, were much more reflective of the Yasu I had encountered at the hotel when I'd dropped the lighter to the ground: savagely aggressive. Instead of reading these rather disconcerting letters over and over again, after one pass I tucked them away.

Who was this boy Yasu? I wasn't sure. I knew very little about him, actually—little beyond the basics, like his birth date and family size. I didn't even know many of his preferences. His writing was nondescript about such things. At this point, I had to reluctantly concede, I was more familiar with Right than with my own purported boyfriend. I knew Right's defining tragedy, along with his position on more topics than I cared to know, and I had heard him describe his homeland many times with great passion.

Right, in all his overbearing protectiveness, elicited a jumble of emotions. He was creepy but caring, judgmental but protective. *Was this the way he was with everyone?*

On Right's last night, on our way back from a trip into town, I decided to address the situation. Pulling over my car to the side of the road a couple of miles from home, I put it into park and confronted Right. I wanted to know, I told him, what was up with him—why he was so emphatic about things involving me and my life. I ask Right why he was always into my business—trying to tell me how to live.

Right paused before replying. "I don't want to see you hurt by stupid people. That's all."

"Damn it!" I thought. I had wanted a teacher, not a savior. I probed a bit further, asking him why he cared so much about me. When I asked whether he cared about me as more than as a friend, he acknowledged that he did. I should never have asked.

Right went on to confess that he wanted to "save" me, to keep me safe from all the bad guys in the world. Finally, he asked point-blank what I thought of him.

I held my head in my hands, having no idea how to respond. Finally, because I couldn't stand the awkward silence, I came out with an inane "Well, I like you too."

This was a lie of sorts. I most certainly didn't "like" Right in the way that might have implied. He was a friend, more of an accidental acquaintance, really. I had met him over a stupid *pen*, of all things!

Then, just as I thought I couldn't possibly sin against my love any more blatantly, I found myself scooting over toward the passenger seat and leaning my head against Right's shoulder.

As I sat there in this ridiculous and compromising position, I realized immediately that there was absolutely no chemistry, nothing at all about the man that had pulled me toward him. Although I couldn't have verbalized this at the time, my move had been calculated. I was afraid of the unknown, fearful in particular of losing all connection to Japan. All I had was a stack of letters from a boy with a one-track mind whom I barely knew. If he were actually using me for his own pleasure—or worse, if he dumped me—I would have nothing to hold on to beyond my broken Japanese dreams.

After instantaneously assessing my situation in terms of risks and benefits, I lifted my head and looked directly at Right. Before I could say anything, he leaned in and kissed me. I responded.

The rest of that night and the next morning were a blur. In front of me stood a mature man who was infusing me with the cultural input I craved; far away was a boy whose straight-out-of-*Playboy* expressions, intoxicating as they were, did little besides scare me. It was entirely possible that Yasu was, as Right would have me believe, playing me.

I made no promises to Right. When he left Michigan our relationship—if indeed it was such—was entirely up in the air. I told him I needed time to think—but the damage had been done. Right Man's disparaging remarks about Yasu pierced through my eardrums. I kept hearing his pronouncements that "only bad guys smoke," "he just wants to play with you," and "he goes to a bad school." Not surprisingly, the content and pacing of my letters changed.

It took Yasu little time to realize something was amiss. In a concerned tone he inquired whether I was busy with schoolwork or if, by chance, I was seeing someone else. Way out there on the other side of the world Yasu had noticed, and I could almost hear his piercing cry calling me to remain focused on him. He wondered on paper what it would take, what he could possibly write that would hold my attention.

In fact, there was nothing Yasu could have done from that distance. My decision had essentially been made when I'd cracked open the door and let Right in. In a "Let's be done with this" moment during one of Right's calls I told him I was his.

I had manufactured my own fate, and the daruma knew it. Every time I walked past the talisman, he appeared to be scowling. When I'd first set him on my dresser, he had appeared jolly, but the chubby little idol, being a temple amulet with spiritual powers, knew exactly what had occurred. I had specifically requested to be with Yasu, but in the end I had been neither patient nor trusting.

CHAPTER 5

Child Prodigy

Mr. Daruma received the pupil in his left eye sometime after I had stopped writing to Yasu. I reasoned that my original wish to see him once again was an extension of my true desire to someday live in Japan. By securing my future with Right, this seemed to have become a foregone conclusion. Unfortunately, the daruma disagreed with my decision and continued with his evil stares—more acute now with his expressive new eyes. Unable to accept his unwaveringly harsh judgment, I eventually cast out my critic and forged ahead without him.

RIGHT PRACTICALLY TURNED ON HIS heels and headed straight back to Michigan after I had told him I was his. In mid-February, just six weeks after he'd left our home, Right returned for a full week. To demonstrate my level of commitment, I gave him the best I had to offer. From that time on he privately called me his wife, and I in turn addressed him as my husband.

Although we weren't together physically during the months that followed, I habitually found myself seated squarely in front of Right, knees bent under my rear, hands pressed palms-down on my thighs, requesting all manner of tutelage. Every day by phone, and sometimes also by letter, Right provided advice on how I was to live my daily life. I was malleable enough that Right could shape me by the simplest suggestion.

Our relationship progressed at a remarkable rate, and within a couple of months of my commitment, Right advised his parents that he planned to marry me, not years later, after he had graduated from college and secured a job, but in a little more than one year, while he was still in school studying on their yen. Understandably, this announcement was less than well received, but in the end Right prevailed. He elicited his parents' reluctant support by cajoling them with the prospect of my helping him following the marriage, both with non-science coursework and with household chores.

In May 1981 Right made the trip to Michigan for the third time—this time including in his luggage a large bag of condoms. During the course of his short stay, he would have me in the woods, in my car, and in our house while my unsuspecting parents slept. The content of Yasu's fantasies, the primary topic of his letters the previous fall, had become my reality with Right. It didn't escape me that Right was no less interested in sex than my "bad boy" had been.

And Right wanted something more. On the last day of his third visit, he revealed his graduation gift to me. As I opened the package with great anticipation, hoping for something from Japan—maybe even from Sado—I was taken aback by the realization that Right's present was something much less unique: a Polaroid camera. This was a puzzling choice from a man who seemed particular about his own photography and owned a nice camera himself. I would soon learn to my consternation that the gift wasn't actually for me.

As I tried to act pleased, Right brought out a couple of accessories—a tripod and some kind of remote trigger device.

"You can take pictures of yourself with this," he announced nonchalantly, as though this bright idea had just occurred to him.

I wondered why I would even want to do such a thing. Right already took plenty of pictures.

He went on, "Well, you can take pictures, and instantly the photo appears. You don't have to take the film to the store to be developed."

I told Right I knew how the camera worked.

"I want you to take some pictures...outside...without clothes."

If I'd been unimpressed by the gift upon opening it, I strongly disliked it now. The ulterior motive of the Polaroid had become all too clear. I informed Right that I couldn't do what he was asking, but he ignored me. Instead, there were more instructions.

"Don't look at the camera…and keep your chin pointing down. That is the 'most cute' pose."

Right always got his way. If I didn't respond well to his request or guidance, he would habitually become sullen and withdrawn. Because he was my sensei, providing instruction on all things, our roles were unequal. "Hai" (*head nod*) "wakarimashita" (*serious face*) became my standard response. "*Yes,*" I nodded in my accustomed agreeable way. "*I understand.*"

Before Japan I had never even considered college, but since Right was a big proponent of higher education and would be in school for the foreseeable future, I decided to go ahead and apply to Michigan State University. My grades, something I'd never cared about, were somehow sufficient, and I was accepted. MSU had no Japanese major at the time, but there were language and humanities courses, and that was where I planned to begin.

Right, having completed his English as a Second Language courses in Louisiana, and having tired of the distance between us, adjusted his original plans to transfer to UC Berkeley's campus and instead headed north. Apparently, however, as smart as my fiancé was, he had not applied his wits to school. His grades were dismally low, and his application to MSU was denied. He would be spending his first year at the local community college.

The distance between us shrank to a few cross-town miles, and with that change the dynamic that had developed over the phone—the "yes, I understand" response Right expected—became deeply embedded in my psyche as the way I needed to behave.

Although I was living in a large dormitory with a roommate and hundreds of other girls my age, I had no time for parties or football games. My fiancé/"husband" was continuously in my space, allowing me literally no time to breathe. Right regularly ate dinner in our cafeteria and slept over most nights, eventually driving my roommate to find a living situation more conducive to her needs.

In the months leading up to our marriage, Right became more critical than ever, frequently advising me that my ways were unbecoming a Japanese bride and that I needed to change. As he clipped and pruned away at my branches and roots, removing aspects of me that in his view served no aesthetic or practical purpose, I held as still as I could, docilely allowing the master gardener to do his work. Naturally this resulted in subtle and not-so-subtle changes in my personal style. Most notably, my speech patterns and expressions changed. Right thought American women were too brazen and brash sounding.

Finally, after nearly two years and many tutoring sessions, the day I had been anticipating arrived. I was returning to Japan, but only for the summer, so I could meet the Chrysanthemum Pond family and Right and I could marry. Right had three more years of undergraduate school remaining.

As we disembarked at Narita, I caught myself thinking about what might have been. Nearly two years earlier, I had been on the departure side of the terminal, examining some gifts I'd just received from friends when by chance I had met the man who was now walking beside me. Had I not received the mechanical pen, it was unlikely Right and I would ever have met. And if we hadn't, Yasu would likely be waiting for me on the other side of baggage claim.

But this was not to be. Yasu was long gone. Not long after Right had moved to Michigan, he'd insisted I quit writing the boy altogether, and although I had received many emotional requests from my old boyfriend to continue corresponding, I did as I was told. Now, instead of meeting up with him and other old friends in Tokyo, I was on my way to the other side of the country and beyond. Sado was not simply another eight or nine hours away; it was another world.

The next morning, as our train to the port city of Niigata lumbered through the Kanto Plain toward the Japanese Alps, I began to experience Sado's "beyond-ness." As the countryside sped past, I began almost tangibly to feel the regression. Each time we emerged from a mountain tunnel, the number of homes with old-school straw roofs seemed to increase. It was as though there were a set of paper doors closing behind us every few kilometers—and with each "new" scene we seemed to reverting back several years. I fully expected to exit the last tunnel and find that the world had regressed to a grainy black and white.

Once in Niigata we boarded a ferry for the two-and-a-half-hour crossing to Sado. More formidable than paper doors, the island's isolation in the sea preserved it. Lounging on the ship's tatami floors, we snacked on Sado delicacies and talked about our big summer plans, until our conversation was interrupted by a crackling loudspeaker announcing that Sado's port had become visible. This was followed by a male vocalist caterwauling to the rhythm of a samisen (a three-stringed, banjo-like instrument) and a large bass drum.

> *"Ah-ah…Sado e to. Sado e to kusa ki mo nabi ku yo!*
> *Sado wa iyoi ka? Sumi yoi ka?"*

> *"Toward Sado. The tree leaves and grasses are blown toward Sado.*
> *Is Sado easy living? Is it a good place to live?"*

There was no welcoming party at the dock because Right's father, an elementary school principal, was away on school business and his mother didn't drive. So our only choice for the last leg of our journey was a cab. Twenty minutes later we began a winding ascent toward the Osado mountain range, and Right advised the driver to look for a small temple on the left. Beyond it was a narrow drive marked by boulders leading up to Right's house.

Exiting the car and seeing Right's mother, I went directly to her and delivered the honorific greeting used for first-time encounters. Satoko bowed in response, acknowledging my request for her favor. While this was happening, Right must have been looking over his mother's shoulder.

"Ba-chan…where's Ba-chan?" he asked, somewhat imperiously, I thought, particularly in light of the length of time since he'd last seen his mother.

"Ah, sore…" Satoko began.

I knew instinctively that her *"Oh, that…"* opener wasn't going to go over well with her son.

Right quickly became agitated, obliging her to be upfront with what she was obviously reluctant to disclose.

"She hasn't been well…her mind, and getting sick easily. Last winter she went to stay in Tokyo…Aunt Junko's house has heat, and we thought it was best."

Right immediately went into accusation mode, alleging that his mother had shipped away his grandmother for some selfish reason.

Before Satoko could get into the details, Right's older sister appeared in the entryway of the house, cradling a tiny baby. Naomi ordinarily lived in Yokohama, but she had returned to her parents' home for a couple of months to give birth and receive postpartum care, as was customary. At the young mother's skirt hem was Miki, Right's almost two-year-old niece whom he'd never met, as she'd been born just after he had left home to study in the United States.

Right nodded coolly toward his sister but like a dog after a bone did not allow her presence to distract him from the more important matter at hand. He informed his mother that he would personally go to Tokyo and retrieve his grandmother before our wedding.

After a few minutes of discussing back and forth the logistics of such a trip, given Ba-chan's condition, Right's mother—or *Ka-chan*, as he called her—requested that the discussion be tabled until *To-chan*, his father, returned. With this Satoko retreated to the kitchen, and we proceeded to take our suitcases inside.

Just as Right had described it—and in contrast to the pocket-sized residences I'd come to know in Tokyo—the house was large and traditional. The main part consisted of six tatami rooms used as bedrooms, a receiving parlor, a tea-drinking/TV room called a *chanoma*, and a formal dining room. Down the north hall was a fireproof tower and two more tatami rooms. The working spaces of the home—the pickling room, sewing area, bath/laundry, kitchen, and informal dining area—were all on the backside of the house alongside a two-story garage containing still even more finished rooms.

All in all it reminded of a miniature samurai castle. More than fifty years old, the farmhouse had been built during Ba-chan's time for her three children. According to Right, his grandmother, a motherless only child, had banished her husband from the family property, divorcing him while the children were still young. She had worked hard to maintain the estate on her own through intensely tough times during the war.

At dinner Right started in on his mother again. He pointed out that, had he known Ba-chan was in Tokyo, he would have picked her up. Satoko tried to explain that such a trip would be too taxing for the old woman, but Right summarily dismissed what he viewed as her excuses. He went on to inform her that, if required, he would go so far as to charter a plane to get his grandmother back. He followed this up by addressing his sister: "*Haven't you become old? Your teeth have rotted since becoming a mother!*" Naomi appeared to be no older than her mid to late twenties. I felt awkward and shocked at the necessity of witnessing this flagrant humiliation.

Jet lag made me the early bird the next morning, or so I thought. As Right slept in, I slipped out the door to check out the house and grounds. In the front garden, I found Satoko, wearing a straw hat and apron, already squatting with her feet flat on the ground. Beside her lay a large scoop made of bamboo. She appeared to be picking weeds from the blanket of moss that covered most of the ground.

"*Ohayo!*" I called out in greeting.

"*Asa hayai desu ne!*" ("[You are] are early riser!"), she responded, seeming pleased that I too was a morning person.

Squatting on tiptoes, I offered assistance. "Shall I help you?"

"After the rain the weeds just pop out!" she explained, standing up and arching her back to stretch. "But I'm almost finished for today." With this she hefted her scoop of weeds and headed toward the garage.

Right had made it clear to me earlier that he disliked his mother. She had worked outside the home when he was young and had left him and his sister in the care of Ba-chan. Naturally, Right had taken to his grandmother and even slept by her side until he was seven. Right said that his mother was prone to violence, yanking her children around by the hair for less than perfect performance, and that his grandmother had protected him as best she could. He insisted that Satoko had always been jealous and was quite evil.

As I walked the pie-shaped property that was bordered by a bamboo forest on one side and the narrow street on another and capped by rice paddies to the north, I couldn't help but notice that the shrubs, pines, and tiny maples had all been meticulously cut and shaped to perfection. Many of the trees were supported by wires to guide their growth.

Under a window stood a row of bonsai trees in small earthenware pots. The small amount of earth around each tiny trunk was blanketed in luscious, bright green moss. As I inspected them more closely, I noticed that many of the trees had been wrapped in copper wire—some branches practically grafting and becoming one with the metal. Standing back to gaze at the whole lot, I found the modified miniature representations of nature beautiful, reminding me of perfect pets.

Right had explained that his family owned their own temple, and—sure enough—there was such a building. As I proceeded to the front of the house, I noticed a small lean-to containing a dozen or more stone Buddhas. Most of the statues were weatherworn to the point of having lost their eyes and noses. Between them were what I presumed to be offerings: coins; a boy's school cap; and, strangely, a naked blond doll with blue crayon scribblings across her face.

I thought, "Of all the temples where someone could place a gaijin doll—a foreign image—why is it sitting prominently in front of our temple naked and defaced?"

For a minute I wondered whether someone had left the doll as an offering in the hope I'd never come. Who knew? Maybe it was "the evil Satoko." Right's professed feelings toward his mother made me cautious.

Leaving behind the defaced-doll mystery, I walked up to the temple building, stuck my hand through the fist-sized hole in the front panel door, and blindly grabbed the braided rope I had expected to find. Upon hearing the muted clang of the bells inside, I let the rope go, put my hands together, and bowed. Acceptance was all I wanted.

Behind the temple were a dozen or more oval stones standing on end—an ancestral burial ground, according to Right. As I walked by each monument looking for the family name among the weatherworn inscriptions, I discovered an old coin. At first I thought I might pick it up and keep it, but when I looked closely I realized that the doubloon had been left in the same spot for a very long time, long enough to wear a crater in the stone.

From the temple area, I wandered through the garage and from there out to the back garden, where I encountered Satoko again, this time carrying a bamboo broom and a long-handled red dustpan. She glanced up at me, smiled, and continued about her work sweeping up a dusting of pine needles I could barely notice. Behind her clean laundry flapped in the breeze. As I looked over the house and grounds, I heard a window slide open.

"*Asa-gohan dekita yo!*" Right's sister called out from the kitchen to let us know breakfast was ready.

Proceeding inside, I smelled the cedar incense burning from the *butsudan*—the indoor altar for the worship of the dead. Instinctively I approached the family altar; hit the small, gold-colored gong with the tiny, baseball-bat-like stick; and then clapped twice and bowed. This was my second prayer of the morning.

As Right continued to sleep, I partook of the elaborate traditional spread with his mother, his sister, and little Miki. As I sat at the low table with my legs folded and tucked beneath my rear, all eyes were on me, anticipating my reactions to each carefully prepared dish.

While I had frequently enjoyed a Western-style breakfast of bread, jam, and milk at Yuki's house, this repast looked more like a dinner. There were sticky beans, broiled fish, and some sort of green jelly cut into noodle-like strips with green onion and soy sauce on top. Determined to show Right's family that I was not some picky foreigner, I ate everything before me.

Over the next few days, Right's *to-chan* (his father, Hideo) returned from his business trip, Naomi went back to Yokohama with her children, and I began to find my place. On a typical day I got up early, ate breakfast with Right's parents, and joined Satoko in bidding "*Itterashai*" ("Good-bye, safe travels") to his father, who worked as an elementary school principal across the valley. Then, if Satoko allowed, I would help her with chores, typically garden work or hanging laundry.

If there was nothing left to do, I would occupy myself and satisfy my natural curiosity through rambling walks. Right almost always slept until around 11:00 a.m., so for a good portion of each day I was free to explore. In my travels I always hoped to encounter neighbors—a handful of children on their way to school or women completing their morning chores. I greeted everyone and sometimes stopped to apprise them of who I was and what I was doing on the island.

This being a close-knit neighborhood, it seemed as though nearly everyone on the hillside already knew of my existence and purpose. But strangely, a couple of times I ran across folks who were evidently mistaken about my association with the community. They would say something like, "Oh, you are American who is going to be the wife of Jinzo!" and I would have to correct them, clarifying, "No, I'm going to be the *yomesan* of Chrysanthemum Pond Right Man."

I was aware that "yomesan" meant both bride and daughter-in-law and that the all-encompassing term was also used by husbands to refer to their wives. But I didn't know the identity of Jinzo or why people seemed to assume I was with him.

Right had apprised me of many things regarding his home, but never once had he mentioned that the house and family line had a name. I finally put two and two together one day when I overheard Satoko answering the phone and took note of her greeting. She answered with a highly attentive voice, saying "*Moshi Moshi*" followed by "*Jinzo de gozaimasu*," which together meant "Hello, hello. This is Jinzo." It was then that I realized that *we* were somehow identified as Jinzo and that I had mistakenly corrected the neighbors in stating that I was not marrying Jinzo's son.

When I asked Right about the strange moniker, he told me it had been the name of some distant ancestor and that it served now as a way to distinguish our household from the other Chrysanthemum Pond households that existed on the island. Apparently Right's last name was the second or third most common on the island, making nicknames like "Jinzo" helpful. Around us lived the Masaemun and Goemun families, and down the street were the Kisaburous—second cousins of Jinzo. None of these were real names; they were pseudonyms derived from more or less distinguished ancestors of record.

My daily free time drew to a close whenever Right found it convenient to rise which was always late. Then, on every fine day, we would leave the house in the early afternoon and head toward some well-known spot.

Along a narrow seaside road known as Sotokaifu, we passed quaint fishing hamlets where squid boats docked; between these we took in surrealistic landscapes of jagged rocks and lush mounds of green, surrounded by water. Japanese tourists poured out of sightseeing buses at every major point of interest—focused on all things quintessentially Sado. In these travels I never saw a fast food restaurant, department store, or any other foreigner like myself.

In the early eighties, time stood still on Sado. If I had liked Japan based on my experiences in Tokyo, I was now infatuated. Sado was not only old but also wildly beautiful. While Tokyo was modern—cooler than America on the basis of all of its ingenious gadgets, a veritable amusement park for the materially insane—Sado was all about culture. There was a history lesson around every corner, and Right took every opportunity to reveal to me the island's greatness.

Since the day I had arrived, we had been in *tsuyuu*—the rainy season. I would have made a tissue ghost had I thought its magical powers would work to stem the drizzle, but in reality the season was both expected and needed. At long last after so many grayed-out days the sun broke through in earnest. That was when Right and I departed to visit Ba-chan. Right was insistent upon going to see his grandmother for himself—not so much in concern for her purported ill health as to assess to his satisfaction whether or not she was fit to ride the trains.

While I had wanted to stay with Yuki for several days and catch up with my Tokyo friends, Right allowed me just one night. His plan was to take me to Yuki's house, stay for the requisite introductions, and then head off to his aunt's house to secure his grandmother's passage.

When Right and I arrived at the Higashi house, everyone was home except Yuki, who was on her way back from class. As we waited Yuki's father engaged Right in conversation, while her mother prepared a feast in the kitchen.

Grandma and Grandpa, both still *genki*—healthy and full of vigor—sat as usual in the TV room. Everyone seemed amused by the fact that Right was from Sado. This was evidently the rough equivalent of hailing from Gettysburg or the birthplace of Lincoln—amplified in significance a hundredfold. Everyone had curious questions about historic sites and life on the island.

Finally, after an hour or so of chitchat, Yuki returned. My sister, cool as a can of milky Calpis, sat silently and listened to Right and her father converse. I knew her well enough to observe that her gears were turning. At one point she even challenged my fiancé on some detail, and the two got into a minor debate that ended with Right's chuckling sarcastically at Yuki. At this Yuki rose, excusing herself to help her mother in the kitchen. By that point I was anxious for Right to take his departure so my sister and I could catch up.

That night Yuki and I reminisced about our summers together. It had been three years since she had stayed with my family in Michigan, and in the relatively short time we had known each other much had changed. Yuki and her high-school friends were scattered among several different universities in Tokyo, and I was about to get married. After getting the scoop on everyone, I dared to ask Yuki her impression of Right.

"What do you think of him?" I asked candidly, knowing full well her opinion would be negative. I wanted to see how much she would divulge.

Yuki averted her eyes. "Oh...I don't know."

In deference to our friendship she was obviously holding back.

"Do you think he's handsome?" This was at the very least a question I thought she could answer, far less personal than asking her impression of his character.

"No, I don't think so."

I dared to brag. "Well, from an American point of view he's good looking. Maybe better looking than Yasu."

In reality I didn't think this. It was just something to say. I waited a few awkward seconds to see whether Yuki had anything more to offer, but "He's not my type" was all she was willing to share.

Yuki's judgment was characteristically quick, and I didn't doubt her. She was far too strong-willed to be with a traditional Japanese man like Right. Quiet and well mannered—perhaps more so than any other Japanese girl I knew—she was too opinionated to be willing to placate.

The next day Right picked me up and took me back to his aunt's place to see his ba-chan. Right's aunt had married a real estate developer and had lived in Tokyo for all of her adult life. As the youngest of three siblings, Aunt Junko was not in any way responsible for Ba-chan's care, but Right's mother had convinced her that the old woman needed to reside in a healthier climate and a warmer, more modern home.

As we waited for Aunt Junko to escort Ba-chan to the tearoom, I asked Right about the old woman's condition.

"Does she remember you?"

"Oh, of course! I am her favorite. She has been sick without me." He turned to look back at Ba-chan. "*Soo deshoo?*" He was asking his grandmother to agree with him.

Worried about whether or not I would be accepted, I asked Right whether he had discussed me with his ba-chan. He assured me that he had.

Just then a petite old woman shuffled slowly into the room on the arm of Aunt Junko. Her dark kimono and jacket had grown too big for her shrinking body. Right rose to his feet and took the arm of his ba-chan from his aunt.

"*Ba-chan ya. Kokochi was doo?*" Right was asking his grandmother how she was feeling.

The old woman's response of "What do *you* want?" indicated that she had already forgotten about seeing Right on the previous day and had no clue who he even was.

Right was immediately attentive, taking his cushion and adding it to the one designated for his grandmother before carefully guiding her to a seating position on the floor. Before replying to Ba-chan's pointed question, he took a few seconds to straighten the front of her kimono. Given her delicate condition and obvious dementia, Right had reluctantly determined that the long train and ferry rides would indeed be too much for her.

A week later, against the wishes of his parents and aunt, Ba-chan arrived home by chartered flight. From the moment she returned to Jinzo, her grandson did everything possible to make sure she was perfectly comfortable. He obsequiously scrutinized her food and accommodations. "Oh, you don't like this cushion, do you, Ba-chan?" he would ask. Or "You would rather watch sumo wrestling, wouldn't you?" Although his grandmother almost never answered his questions, Right acted as a mind reader in order to make her world as perfect as possible.

Right's doting attention to Ba-chan created friction in the house. In her son's eyes nothing Satoko did was good enough. Oblivious to everything, including the commotion surrounding her, Ba-chan invariably seemed content to sit in silence. Only once did I hear her speak up, and that was to defend me in front of her grandson after he had forced me to select a particular kimono fabric over another I preferred. Ba-chan, who had been present for the entire exchange, later instructed Right to amend the custom order to my preference. Perhaps she resented a man telling a woman what she should wear. *In that moment Right's grandmother reminded me of Yuki—like my sister, wise and tough.*

August was a busy time in *furusato* towns and villages, places considered "homelands" to folks living in cities. During the early part of the month, families living in rural areas like Sado prepared their gravesites and temples for Obon, the annual worship of the dead that was to occur mid-month. Once these preparations were complete, the country folk would host their city counterparts, who would pour out of trains and busses not only to worship but to enjoy a time of respite from their hectic city lives. We had arranged for our wedding to take place directly after Obon so that family members wouldn't have to travel separately for the festivities—making the time extra busy for Hideo and Satoko.

It was mid-preparation that To-chan and Ka-chan left the island. Hideo was in the process of cutting down select bamboo trees and fashioning flower holders out of their shafts, but before he could finish this work he announced that they would have to depart for a few days. Right had insisted that his parents go after the other driver involved in his motorcycle accident in 1979, and somewhere on the other side of the main island a court case was pending. It was for Right's retribution they felt obliged to take their leave at this inopportune time.

During his parents' absence, Right and I played house. He taught me a few things in the kitchen, but for the most part he did the cooking while I occupied myself with table setting and cleanup duties. Even though my assigned tasks were simple, Right scrutinized my every move for quality and efficiency; this was a boot camp of sorts.

If I thought I knew how to wipe down a table or wash dishes, I learned that I was mistaken. A wiping cloth had to be folded into a neat square and a clean surface of the cloth exposed every wipe or two. And I couldn't run a sink full of water to wash dishes. Instead I had to dip each one into a pan of hot water and wash them off to the side.

Within those few days, I made many mistakes in terms both of sequence and of mannerisms. Exhibit One among my indiscretions was an incident involving a piece of my own dirty clothing. I had noticed a stain on a pair of white capris, and Right was in a position to easily place them in a pan of detergent for soaking. Instead of asking Right kindly whether or not he would mind accepting my dirty clothing and then holding out the item for his retrieval, I tossed the capris in his direction while making the request, as in, *"Hey, would you mind putting these in that soapy pan of water over there?"* (toss).

In response to my grave dual mistakes of assuming and then tossing without warning, Right "cleared" the dinner table with one swoop, leaving me to clean up the mess. It was in this way I learned not only to never assume but also to be wary of the potential consequences of any mistake. Japanese tableware doesn't break into pieces that can be easily gathered up; it *explodes* into thousands of sliver-like shards.

By the time Right's parents returned from attending to the legal matters, I was feeling rather oppressed and was more than ready to get outside and dance. And just in time for the Obon festivals my custom *yukata* arrived. I modeled the summer kimono, tying my own obi sash as Yuki had taught me when she had first come to the United States.

Right's mother expressed surprise at how elegant I looked and was doubly impressed by my obi tying skills. She for whatever reason did not choose to advise me, however, that the bow configuration I had chosen was for maidens and that after I was married I would have to master a new tying method.

Attending my first Obon dance alone, I tried my hand at Sado Okesa under the curious eyes of neighbors and other townspeople. I repeated the sixteen steps over and over again, swaying to the beat of a large drum and waving my hands to mimic the sea. For my first rendition, I won a set of summer teacups and for the second, a fat round watermelon.

Following Obon, exactly two years to the day after my meeting Right Man, we were married. In front of Right's parents and my own—from whom I'd hidden much of my difficulty, and who were in any case not the type to intervene—with both of our paternal grandmothers in attendance, both Right and I swallowed three sips of sake from each of three cups to signify the union, Shinto style. Although Right's family was Buddhist, Japanese marriages were almost always performed according to rituals established by Japan's native religion.

The wedding was small, but nearly a hundred guests, mostly neighbors, attended the reception at the finest hotel on the island. One can only imagine how I looked, what with my black lacquer *geta*—platform flip flops that consisted of flat wooden footboards elevated by two crossbar heels—and heavy "wedding do" wig adding a good six inches to my height, already more than imposing by Japanese standards. But even with my basketball player stature, I was able to pull off the look and remain poised. Many people complimented me on how Japanese I looked, and I can only report that "a good time was had by all."

On that day my name was officially added to Jinzo's record. Not only was I a member of the household, I was *yomesan* to the only heir—tasked with ensuring that the estate would be preserved and the line carried forward. How exactly this was to occur I had no clue, but I was completely dedicated to the cause. A few days later Right said good-bye to his dear ba-chan, and we returned to Michigan.

CHAPTER 6

The House of Jinzo

In traditional Japanese homes, there is a good deal riding on the eldest son. He is the one who typically stands to receive the entire inheritance; in turn, he is responsible for taking care of the aging parents. If one is from a furusato—the location at which the ancestors sleep—the chonan (eldest son) has the additional responsibility of caring for generations past.

When there is no backup plan—no other son or willing daughter— the expectations fall squarely upon this one individual, designated by birth and gender. This was Right's position, and it was to become mine.

ALTHOUGH I WAS AT THE time of our marriage a nearly nineteen-year-old American whose family line was as convoluted as any other in the West, whose ancestry consisted of a hodgepodge of immigrants from the British Isles, the gravity of the situation—the weight of Jinzo—did not escape my awareness. In fact, I relished the idea of living with the import of all the history and the grave responsible for the legacy. This was an absolutely positive aspect of the package in my eyes.

As someone who had grown up in the countryside with parents who be-lieved in long chore lists, I'd been raised to be a hard worker. And I have little doubt that Satoko and Hideo noticed my abilities. If they were skeptical when

I arrived, after two weeks it didn't show. Morning by morning as their son slept in, I was outdoors following them around, asking what they were doing and trying to learn.

Satoko shared with me on several occasions that her son was lazy and never helped them. She implored me to be a good influence—to make sure he studied and did well in school. I assured her I would: *"Hai. Ganbarimasu"* (*"Yes. I will try my best"*).

Far away, as Hideo and Satoko prayed at their altar and maintained the graves, I have no doubt they worried. They had only one son, and their daughter was married off to another *chonan*, the eldest son of another family from another place.

Right and I settled ourselves into Michigan State University's married housing and began our sophomore years together. Unsure of what I wanted to be other than a Japanese housewife, I continued to study Japanese language and culture, while Right settled in to his physics program. We took our general education classes together so I could help Right study and complete papers. In turn, Right helped me continue to grow in my knowledge of all things Japanese.

First on the list of things I needed to know was how to cook, Japanese-style. My own mother cooked only the most basic dishes—typical American fare that included lasagna; sloppy Joes; and a bland soup she called "macaroni and milk" that consisted of elbow pasta, powdered milk, butter, salt, and pepper—and she had never taught me anything related to meal preparation.

In the early eighties, Asian groceries were hard to come by in Michigan, but Satoko would occasionally send us a sea-mail box of dried ingredients: various types of seaweed, fish stock, shiitake mushrooms, and noodles. And Right had skills; during some of his high-school and college-prep-school years he had lived away from his parents and had taken care of himself. He was able to use whatever we received from Japan, in conjunction with local meats and vegetables, to create homemade dishes that rivaled any I had eaten on Sado.

Right would measure and taste over and over again, and when he determined an optimal combination he would write out a recipe card for me. These instructions—complete with details like vegetable washing techniques and proper cutting illustrations—were painstakingly written out in Japanese. Little by little I became able to use the recipes and cook a few things to my husband's satisfaction.

Over time I developed a repertoire that included yakisoba fried noodles made from thin spaghetti and donburi rice bowl meal, using hamburger and cabbage. Right would ask me at every meal whether or not I had followed his recipe, and I felt obliged to say I had, whether or not I had actually checked the card, as opposed to having measured based on memory. Even after the fact of writing out the recipe cards, my husband was continuously tweaking the recipes—rebalancing saltiness and sweetness with more or less soy sauce, brown sugar, and sake.

Using only chopsticks in conjunction with small plates and rice bowls, we ate Japanese fare most of the time. Outfitted with a low table Right had crafted out of two-by-fours and sitting on flat pillows made from special "husband blue and wife pink" cushion fabric Satoko had sent, our university apartment looked like any properly outfitted *chanoma* or sitting parlor.

Besides teaching me how to cook, Right instructed me on housekeeping (which is taught in Japanese schools; instead of using janitors, the children clean) and personal hygiene. He liked things to be impeccably clean and was especially meticulous in the kitchen and obsessive on the issue of hand washing. He was continuously asking me whether or not I had washed my hands after entering the apartment and before I touched any food. I learned to run the water full force so he could *hear* my hand washing clearly enough for me to avoid being asked. If Right thought a plate or piece of food had in any way been touched by an unclean object, he wouldn't hesitate to throw it out.

Most of the time, I was able justify my husband's compulsive strictness based on my knowledge of how black and white Japanese people tend to be. From the old samurai movies to modern daytime dramas, male characters are invariably strong and dramatic. The kinds of statements from Right that had so disconcerted me upon my initial exposure—the "this is good" and "that is bad" generalities—were typical of the straightforward Japanese. My own unique role, scripted to fall somewhere between that of the cute young idols of our time and traditional leading ladies, was to speak softly and respond with a "Yes, I understand" level of obedience to my man.

The traditional and unspoken sensei/grasshopper roles (as in the *Kung Fu* TV show) allowed Right to wield power over me; when I failed to answer appropriately I would be berated and left alone to *hansei*, or reflect. As had happened on that unexpectedly memorable occasion on Sado when I had mistakenly thrown my stained capris toward Right without first asking his favor, more serious transgressions resulted in breakage—an almost systematic loss of dishes, knickknacks, or whatever else might have been at hand. Sometimes Right would go so far as to rip the clothes from my body and tear them into shreds.

While simple reprimands would have been sufficient to correct my course, Right invariably added layers of gravity to any situation—at least ostensibly, lest I forget. On top of the violence, I noticed that my mistakes tended to have a lingering negative effect on his studies. If I did anything wrong at all, my passive-aggressive husband would retaliate with a refusal to crack his books. I had developed a habit of noting the position of every text, paper, and pencil on Right's desk. On too many days nothing was moved. Aware that Right had done poorly in high school and had subsequently failed several entrance exams, I was fearful of his failing courses and dropping out. This was a burden Ka-chan had carried for many years, and now it had become mine. I began to feel the pressure of the Jinzo legacy bearing down upon me. Right had to make it; he had to succeed so that the estate might be preserved and the souls of the ancients find rest.

If I could make it through an entire day without committing an indiscretion, Right would tell me several times that he loved me and call me Boo-chan—his pet name for me. If I were "good" several days in a row, he would even buy me a treat or small toy. Being good had a lot to do with acting childlike, all the while performing tasks precisely, as an adult. This was all an infuriating balancing act. By the end of our first year together, I cried more than I smiled.

From the very beginning, I had entertained first subtle and then grave doubts, but two and a half years into my relationship with Right I began to harbor some serious ill will toward him. As these feelings continued to escalate, I recalled the "boy" with whom I had initially been so smitten and wondered what had become of him. It was in this state that one day, while Right was attending classes, I managed to purchase a car, pack my things, rent an apartment, and skedaddle, leaving not so much as a note. No longer would I have to wash my hands a hundred times a day or fear losing property as retribution for simple mistakes.

Even in my liberated state I didn't go wild; instead I remained mostly alone, thinking of Japan and how I could get back there. I had no plans for returning to my pre-Japanese days but remained intent on forging ahead with my all-consuming pursuit of choice. I yearned to experience on my own the place I had come so to love, equipped as I was now with vastly improved abilities in all things Japanese. If possible, I wanted a do-over. And as hard as I had tried, I'd never forgotten Yasu's address.

By this time my Japanese was surely better than Yasu's English, and it most certainly expressed the subtle nuances I wanted to convey.

"*I'll be in Japan again this summer. If you have time, would you like to meet up?*" I wrote, hoping my short note would reach him.

Two weeks later I received Yasu's reply. After the requisite opening paragraph (*a brief description of weather conditions in his locale*), Yasu answered the all-important question: "*Yes, I want to see you again. However, you cannot stay at my house.*"

I hadn't asked to stay at his house, so I took this as Yasu's way of cautioning me that our meeting would be as friends. This was what I had expected. It was at least a start.

I spent the next couple of weeks planning my adventure. Secretly I had saved the charm necklace Yasu had given me at Kurohime camp and started wearing it. I skipped around the apartment, knowing I would see my first love again. But just when I thought I was free, Right found my apartment.

I had taken precautions to stay away from areas Right frequented, but somehow he had managed to locate me. He looked pitiful, as though he'd been through hell, and I couldn't help but feel a tinge of sympathy. Still I held my ground, refusing to allow him past the threshold of my apartment and deflecting his pleas for me to return. He informed me that Jinzo was unaware of my departure, that he was keeping the secret in the hope I would return.

The next day I received an unexpected call. On the other end of the line was Yasu's mother.

"Please do not bother my son," she requested, adding, "He has a fiancé. Your visit would be bothersome."

I was in shock. The rest of that day and through the night I weighed my options, trying to decide whether or not to proceed with the trip. The next morning I received a second call from Japan, this time from Yasu.

I asked him straight up whether what his mother said was true, and he admitted that it was. Denouncing his mother's interference, however, Yasu asked me to stick with my plans and visit him. He wanted to meet me. I told him I was undecided.

As was customary, our conversation had to end on a good note, so I switched topics and asked Yasu whether he was in school.

"I study bookkeeping. But my head is bad. Every day I think *ahhh!*" he admitted, laughing at his lack of ability. It was refreshing to hear a Japanese man admit to a deficit in any area. Yasu's humble honesty reminded me of why I had been attracted to him in the first place.

"*Ganbatte!* Yasu (try your hardest!)" I urged.

Yasu encouraged me to do the same, tacking on, "Come to Kawasaki, okay?"

I didn't know how to respond. My do-over hopes had been dashed by the fact that he was planning to marry.

It was difficult for me to decipher the motivation behind Yasu's call. If he had a fiancée, why would he want me around? I was certain there would be a crazy tension if I were to show up. Someone was bound to be hurt, and chances were *I'd* be that someone.

Not long after I hung up the phone, while I remained in my indecisive stupor, Right showed up again. This time I let the pitiful soul in.

The next morning I awoke to sunlight streaming through my window. I lay still for a while, trying to recall where I was and what I was supposed to be doing that day. Then, with a sinking feeling, I remembered the call from Yasu. A wave of disappointment came over me—followed immediately by a startling recollection: I had allowed Right to stay the night.

Still in a daze over what had happened the night before, I stumbled into the bathroom and stood at the vanity, staring at my reflection. As I gazed into the mirror, I suddenly remembered having stashed Yasu's necklace and recent letter under the sink when I realized Right was at my door. Knowing intuitively that something was wrong, I groped beneath the sink. Not surprisingly, the letter and necklace were gone.

I dressed and headed out to look for Right. As I approached my car, I could see shattered glass on the car seat and the floor, remnants of our framed wedding picture. Yasu's letter and chain lay near it. I tossed the broken glass, the letter, and the chain into a nearby Dumpster before speeding off.

I found Right in his campus apartment lying on his bed, face up. His eyes were wide open, but he refused not only to talk but to acknowledge my presence in any way. Over and over again I told him how sorry I was, adding that my feelings for Yasu had been rekindled only because our marriage had not been going well. Nothing had been gained by my leaving.

Shortly after my return to Right, I called my mother to ask whether we could come by. I could sense reluctance on her part, but she agreed, saying we should come on Sunday when my father was around. They were aware that I had separated from my husband, and since that time I had shared a good deal with them. I thought it might be helpful for Right and me to visit them together and show them our new, united front.

As we entered the house, I caught a glimpse of my little sister, moving fast. She was all but a blur as she ducked into her lower-level bedroom. I called out, but the only response was the sound of her door closing and the lock turning. I found this odd, though my sister wasn't particularly social. Brushing off the incident, I proceeded with Right up the stairs of our bi-level to the main living area.

The house was eerily quiet. No one had come to the door or called out to us. Right took a seat in the living room while I made my way around to the kitchen, where I found my mother standing at the sink. She was tight-lipped and cold, and I was uncertain what to make of her mood.

Taking a seat at the breakfast bar, I watched my mother wipe the counters and scrub the stovetop. Bored, I began absentmindedly to finger through some papers stacked nearby. Among the junk mail and bills was a handwritten envelope—and underneath it a letter. The penmanship belonged to Right. My chin dropped. My mother was ready to talk.

"Yeah! Look at that!" she acknowledged in a sarcastic tone, throwing down her towel, hard, on the countertop. "Do you know he actually delivered this piece of crap to your *sister* at school?"

I was puzzled, absolutely confused as to what she might be trying to tell me. I asked which day.

"A couple of days ago. Thursday, it was." My mother's tone was clipped.

He must have skipped classes to do it. Thursday had been a busy day for him. I looked over at the living room chair, where Right had been sitting. He had disappeared.

My mother looked me square in the eyes. "Did you know he felt that way about your sister?" she asked point-blank.

"He told me he thought she was cute and that she was a nice girl," I replied tentatively, still uncertain where this was going. I had confronted him about the issue a couple of times, but he had chastised me for making something of nothing.

At that point my mother, unhinged now, started to screamed rapid-fire questions at me across the breakfast bar.

"Read the letter! Read the whole sick thing. Did he actually think she wouldn't tell us about this? Did he think she would respond to his advances?"

Feeling ill, I skimmed each page. The first few contained a prolonged declaration of his feelings for my sister. Further into the letter, he wrote about me and his fear that I would hurt her if I were to learn the truth about his love. One sentence—"*I wish you were small like a doll so I could carry you in my pocket and protect you*"—stuck out. The letter was signed "Your Poor Brother."

I looked back toward the living room. Right was nowhere to be seen. Was he looking for my sister—his desired little toy?

A couple of minutes later Right reappeared in the living room. Realizing that the situation was about to get much worse, I picked up my purse and informed Right in a monotone that I thought we should go. My mother was still standing in the kitchen, her hands on her hips. Clearly aghast, she asked how in the world I could bring myself to leave with him.

"Mom, I have to hear his side," I told her in a placating voice, all the while moving toward the door. Right was well ahead of me; I was actually trying to catch up.

Exasperated, my mother followed. "*His side?* He's a dirty-minded SOB!"

"Listen, our relationship hasn't been good. I myself had fantasies about someone else. I kind of understand why Right's mind may have wandered."

I said this as though I were intending to forgive, but his words describing his attraction toward my sister really cut. At that point I blurted what must have come out as a disjointed string of confused and angry words: It wasn't *my* fault I had been in an accident. If I hadn't been injured maybe I would even have been somewhat pretty…looked more normal…more like my sister. I was the one who had the scars. Why didn't he want to save *me*?

My mother couldn't believe her ears.

"I don't care! This is your sister we are talking about here! She's only fifteen! He's writing about falling for her when she was thirteen!"

I reminded my mother that I had been sixteen when I'd first met Right. Fifteen wasn't much of a difference.

"Stacy! How can you do this? You're making a huge mistake. The man is in love with your *sister!* You can't possibly live with him!"

I walked out, leaving my mother standing at the door yelling after me. She had resorted to threats…to call the cops…to have him deported…whatever it might take…

All the way home, Right's written expressions of love toward my sister replayed like a macabre tape in my mind. If he had written to a stranger, someone my age, I could easily have dismissed the letter as a tit-for-tat re-sponse to my summertime infatuation with Yasu. But he had written to my own sister—to an unscarred, younger, more perfect version of myself.

When I confronted Right, he had the gall to be indignant. Beauty, he informed me in a dispassionate tone, was in the eye of the beholder, and preferences, despite age, couldn't be helped. My sister was cute; her age was irrelevant to that fact. It went without saying that he would never touch her. He was just letting her know how special she was—assuring her he was there to protect her.

CHAPTER 7

Cruel Gardener

I was not even twenty, but I was aging at a rapid rate. Right had once let slip to me that Playboy *models were "too old"—and when we were on Sado he had made that odd comment about his own sister, who had not yet reached thirty, looking like an old woman. "Iiko iiko" ("good girl"). As much as possible I had to remain just that. I thought I had been a decent person for most of my life, but being an* iiko *required absolute obedience—a level of rule-following to which Americans would never subscribe. This was a foreign concept, but I was starting to get it.*

I SLIPPED BACK INTO MY dutiful housewife role as quickly as I had left it. Right's fall term was underway, and he needed to succeed. Every day I put on my apron and, at our makeshift *genkan* entry, where our shoebox and a square piece of plastic covering the carpet separated the "dirty" shoe area from the rest of the living space, squatted with bent knees, passing my husband his hot *bento* box filled with Japanese-style homemade delicacies as he prepared to depart for his physics and math classes.

Understandably, the letter to my sister had destroyed any semblance of even the tenuous relationship Right may have managed to maintain with my family. My parents had witnessed my husband's overbearing behavior firsthand—both with me and toward his own mother during their brief stay on Sado for our wedding. During a time I should have been budding into a young woman, I was slipping backward, regressing before their eyes. Although they had always harbored concerns about Right, they had put up with him for my sake. Now they had every reason to cut him out of their lives.

Right was perfectly content with the situation. He had from the beginning written off my family as "low class" and a negative influence, blaming my parents for my unpolished behavior and even for the car accident of so long ago.

Since he was now banned from my parents' house, Right saw it as his prerogative to ban me from seeing them. When I informed my parents of the new rules my normally "hands off" father was pushed to the breaking point. One day, on his way in to work, he unexpectedly burst into our university apartment, pinned Right against a wall, and accused him of not knowing how to treat a woman.

Following this incident I was all but isolated in my Japanese world away from Japan.

Having no friends and barred from contact with my own parents, I lived the life of an exile in our small apartment. For nearly a thousand years poets, playwrights, and political figures at odds with whatever regime happened to have been in power had been banished to Sado. The famous exiles were put under house arrest, while the common criminals and homeless individuals were forced to work in the gold mine. I could imagine such characters, alone with their thoughts, going out of their minds.

By this time I had been trimmed and shaped for three years, like one of the transplanted bonsai trees Hideo kept in Jinzo's garden. Although I appreciated the fact that I had become more "Japanese" than ever, my sanity was at risk. I was often accused of things I hadn't done, but Right was so convincing I began to question whether I knew anything at all. Maybe I didn't even know myself. During this time my mental state continued to deteriorate.

I developed a habit of striking my forehead whenever Right was angry with me. To pound my head with my fists seemed to befit my crime of stupidity. There were variations—hitting my head against the headboard or wall or substituting objects at hand. I unwittingly experimented with various ways to hurt myself, but head banging seemed to be my preference.

Right ignored my bad—and in his eyes irrelevant—habit. What was important to him was that I understood my crimes sufficiently to fix them. One day during my *hansei*, my post-misbehavior reflection time, I became hysterical and found myself unable to recover. Utterly unable to stem the flood of my tears, I drove myself to the campus medical center, where after a series of interviews I was detained, strapped down, and taken by police cruiser to a city hospital.

As I sat in the waiting room with my assigned guard, I started thinking through my situation. A part of me longed to be locked up—away from Right—and cured of whatever it was that was causing me so much misery, but as I thought through the possible scenarios if I were committed, I realized I wasn't quite crazy enough for so drastic a step. Despite my desperation I retained the ability to think through paths and outcomes.

As I waited to be evaluated, I decided I could and should pull myself together. I managed to pass the tests administered to me and was released. This incident was pivotal. It may have been, I decided, that channeling all of my effort into pleasing Right was making me so nervous it was causing me to make more mistakes than I would otherwise have done. What I needed was more confidence, not less.

"Keep your chin up in class, your chin down at home. Find the balance." This became my mantra.

That fall I declared a major and signed up for a full load. Among the classes I had taken with Right were several introductory philosophy courses. These had become my favorites. I loved the logic of syllogisms and enjoyed the in-class debates. When I informed Right that I wanted to study philosophy, he was surprisingly pleased. He thought this would be a good foundational major similar to his physics—a discipline that would help me differentiate, after the manner of a good Japanese wife, *ii koto* from <u>*warui koto*</u>—good things from bad.

A mediocre student in high school, I'd never expended much effort when it came to bookwork—with the exception, of course, of my Japanese studies, but over the next two semesters I studied incessantly and received perfect grades in return for my efforts. I did this not only because I found that I could but because I thought Right would be impressed.

In 1985 Right earned his bachelor's degree. Given the caliber of his grades, I had thought this might be the end of the road for him, but somehow he managed to convince two of his professors to recommend him for graduate school, and this decision worked well for me. Despite the fact that we had started college at the same time, my household duties and shaky mental state had left me more than a year behind him in school.

I thought that with Right's new plan we would remain in Michigan for another two years—long enough for me to graduate—but this wasn't meant to be. Shortly after starting the fall semester, Right abruptly dropped out of school. I was uncertain why he had quit but surmised that somehow he had gotten behind and/or found the advanced coursework too difficult. What he told me was that he wanted to go back to Sado and see his ba-chan. He sensed that something was amiss, that his parents were being less than truthful about her condition. While I thought his concerns were legitimate, given the depth of his adoration, I also suspected that Right may have become tired of school.

With this abrupt change in our course, I too dropped out of school and prepared for the biggest move of my life. By this time it had been six years since Yuki had stayed with my family, five since I had first traveled to Japan, and a little more than three since we had married. It went without saying that the time away from the true object of my affection had been entirely too long.

In Michigan, in our constraining university apartment, I had been a pretender. I was living a completely Japanese life within our four walls, but in doing so I had become for all intents and purposes an expatriate in my country of origin. Not only had my speech and mannerisms been affected, but my thought processes had been significantly altered as well. I had come to the point of thinking in another language, of viewing everything through an alternative cultural lens, and it seemed to be the time to put everything I'd learned to the test.

Right was prepared to return to Japan and get on with his life, and I was ready to test my greatly enhanced Japanese wife skills. But before we could leave, he wanted to purchase a few items that wouldn't be readily available in Japan—pornography to be exact, which apparently was illegal, at least in the sense that the most private areas in a photograph had to be blurred or covered with a black strip. This regulation pertained to all types of material, including magazines, comics, and movies. Right had regularly purchased commemorative issues of *Playboy* and had borrowed videos during his time in the United States. Because he wouldn't have the same opportunities in Japan, he decided to go on a copying spree.

After spending a couple of weeks making numerous trips to the x-rated shops and holed up with his video recorders between these forays, Right was ready to go. I would stay on in Michigan to clean up the apartment and ship our belongings.

When Right had first come to the United States, he had planned to earn a master's degree or doctorate in physics and to work in a college-research environment, but since he was returning to rural Sado with a bachelor's degree in science he had no idea what type of job he could secure. Even so, finding employment was not in the forefront in his mind. Right obsessed about Ba-chan beyond what might have been considered normal. Hideo and Satoko had indicated by letter and phone calls that her condition had further deteriorated.

Soon after Right returned to Sado, he called with terrible news: unbeknownst to either of us, his beloved grandmother had been placed in a nursing home shortly after our wedding. Right suspected that his parents had withheld this information on the assumption that the old woman would pass before he could return and discover the truth. He estimated now that she wouldn't last more than a few weeks in her frail condition. Right suggested that I stay for the time being in Michigan, since he had little interest in being around his parents once his grandmother was gone.

I was dumbfounded. Just that day I had shipped a dozen large tangerine boxes by sea mail. How could the situation have gone so unexpectedly awry?

"My parents didn't take care of her." Right said squarely placing blame.

I surmised immediately that Right had been arguing with them. Ba-chan's "involvement" in the lives of the family, such as it was, invariably precipitated vicious verbal conflict.

Right explained that since his arrival back on the island he had been attending to her at a *ryojinhomu* (nursing home) across the valley—spoon-feeding her every meal in an apparently futile attempt to stimulate and revive her withering spirit.

Right was clearly shaken, and I tried to support him from afar, reassuring him how good it was that he was there for his ba-chan. My thoughts couldn't help but wander, though, to what was going to happen next.

"Do you have ideas about work?" I broached the subject gingerly.

Right had never worked; from my understanding he'd never so much as taken a small cash job or earned money for a chore. I was worried that he might be unemployable.

"Ba-chan is going to die. My parents are terrible." Right blurted sullenly, sidestepping my question.

I explained the obvious to Right: everyone dies, and with advancing age, decline and eventually death are expected. But this was clearly not what Right wanted to hear. He reiterated that Ba-chan's current state was entirely due to his parents' scandalous neglect. At that moment I was thankful to be beyond his reach.

"Are you going to stay or return to Michigan?" I asked.

My own destiny lay in the balance. I needed clarity. Ba-chan was eighty-six. What could he possibly be expecting?

"I got some books to study for a teacher's license. My parents said there is a teacher shortage and I can get a temporary certificate."

Somehow I doubted Right was studying. By now I knew his modus operandi—his MO. Over the years Hideo and Satoko had shipped their son a veritable library of dictionaries and physics books, all of which remained in mint condition, like new. Right liked having a shelf full of texts on heady subjects, but he rarely cracked any of these tomes. *Was he really studying anything at all?*

Pretenses, I thought grimly. The books in his hands are just for appearances.

"*Ganbatte*," I urged him—the standard "give it effort" Japanese response. My saying anything more would have been construed as parental and hence completely maddening to Right.

Toward the end of our conversation, my husband seemed to relax. He would be staying for the time being and would try to acquire some kind of teaching job.

As I hung up the phone, my Japanese life flashed before me. What on earth had I done? I had invested so much into my Japanese future, and it was all in Right's hands. Whatever it took, I had to convince him that staying in Japan and living on Sado, however meager his earnings, would be best for both of us. Right was far too Japanese to assimilate into the culture of my birth—and I had worked so hard to become a part of his.

PART II

My Root-Bound Days

CHAPTER 8

Bent People and the Brother-Son

It was January 1986, and I was in Japan for the third time—not for a visit but presumably for the rest of my life. Through years of strict training I'd held fast to my Japanese dream.

IT WAS MY FIRST TIME in Japan during the winter, and Tokyo was rather dreary. I was alone for this trek, and happily so—proficient enough to get around on my own and, without Right's continuous scrutiny, feeling momentarily liberated.

Only one major change had become evident in my absence: the trip to Sado had become considerably shorter, cut nearly in half by the installation of a new bullet train known as the Joetsu Shinkansen. I had seen its elevated rails alongside the old express tracks four years earlier, before it was up and running. The new train would take travelers to Niigata in record time, making Sado far less remote.

This fact made me a little bit sad; still, fast or slow, all that really mattered was that I was back—and back in a big way. Finally, after all my formal and informal study, I was ready on my own to take on life in Japan.

And this time I was enthusiastically welcomed. Hideo and Satoko, unaware of our struggles in Michigan, seemed glad to see me when I arrived at their door. I had been a mere child when they had last seen me—a perceived appendage to their son's potential success, but—*thanks to me*—Right had graduated on time and had safely returned. In fact, after dinner that first evening Satoko pulled me aside and thanked me for taking care of her son's *mendou*, his "trouble." This was a common expression, typically stated as a matter of courtesy, but the emphasis in her voice clued me in that she meant it. Following this she expressed with a double wink what we both already knew: that her son was a selfish boy, adding that recently Right had been throwing his weight around on the touchy subject of getting Ba-chan back home. My impression was that Satoko was looking to me for sisterhood.

The next morning Right got up uncharacteristically early, grabbed the equivalent of twenty dollars from his mother's change purse, and left with me for the *ryojinhomu*. To-chan, knowing his son would expect to use the family car, walked a mile or so down the hill to town to catch a bus for work. The nursing home was about twenty-five minutes down the hill and across the valley, in Satoko's hometown of Mano.

At the home's main entrance, we traded in our shoes for vinyl slippers before proceeding down a large, open hallway. As we scuffled along, we came upon a woman dressed in a traditional nurse's outfit, complete with a winged white cap. The nurse recognized Right and quickly introduced herself—*after* the usual "You are so tall!" exclamation directed toward me.

Right's grandmother was in a room with three other ba-chans, their state of decline evidenced by their lack of reaction to my unaccustomed entrance. One ba-chan sat with her mouth wide open, and another lay incapacitated. The third was meticulously engaged in picking at an imaginary something from her quilt. Our grandmother, no better, appeared not to recognize me at all.

Right was patient with his grandmother's lunchtime feeding, asking her to "open up" several times before getting in a single bite. Every time she took a spoonful of the runny rice topped with salmon flakes he would praise her. This was an endearing side of Right I rarely saw.

For the evening meal, Right insisted that Ba-chan get out of bed; he lifted her himself into her wheelchair and wheeled her to the lounge, where two other ba-chan were already eating. Right knew their names and introduced them to me as Fujiwara-san and Nakagawa-san. Both were mentally spry, and their reaction to me was similar to that of the nurse. Since Right was solicitous in his care of Ba-chan, I decided to make conversation with the ladies, both cheerful women I liked instantly. Before their return to their rooms each insisted I eat her dessert custard.

We arrived back at Jinzo in time for our dinner. A kerosene heater was running to keep us comfortable while we ate, but the house was oppressively cold. At any given time two or three kerosene heaters were running, but most rooms had no heat whatsoever, and I had seen snow indoors, having blown in through cracks between the walls. I dreaded leaving the warmth of the dining area and took to wearing multiple layers under a quilted kimono jacket.

I was quickly caught up in the predictable routine of traveling back and forth between our house and Mano. Right was relentless in his care, and since I wasn't needed at Ba-chan's bedside I took to chatting up the two old ladies, both of whom took pleasure in trying to fatten me up.

These women were seasonal residents of the home, having come for cold-weather respite from their mountain abodes. Fujiwara-san was cute as a button, her doll-like face reminding me of Yuki's. Over time I learned that her husband had passed and that she had become affiliated with an "arranged family" of sorts. Her "son" was actually a younger brother who had been grafted into her household years earlier when she had failed to conceive. Nakagawa-san was one of the "bent people"—when she stood the upper part of her body was nearly parallel to the floor, and when she walked she found it necessary to stop every few steps, lean on her staff, and tilt her head backward to see where she was going. The condition, I learned, was caused by a combined calcium deficiency and a lifelong history of fieldwork.

Through my conversations with these women, my ability to understand Sado dialect improved greatly. These two dear souls constituted my claim to sanity during the eight-hour shift Right and I voluntarily covered at the nursing home.

A month or so had gone by when I was advised that a certain holiday was approaching. I had been unaware of any February events on the Japanese calendar but was given to understand that the third day of the month, Setsubun, would involve an exorcism of sorts. That evening Hideo brought forth two wooden boxes of beans, explaining their intended use for expelling demons. Following his instructions I made my way throughout the house, tossing the beans out of doorways and windows while yelling *"Oni wa soto...fuku wa uchi"* ("Demons out! Luck in!").

While Hideo and Satoko may secretly have wished that their son would on the basis of this ritual come to his senses and realize that Ba-chan was already in the right place, given her condition and the excellent facilities available in town, this did not happen. Shortly after Setsubun Right had an announcement to make.

It was late, and the four of us were seated at the dinner table when Right told his parents that he would be bringing his grandmother home. He had obtained permission from the nursing home doctor, and her scheduled release date was less than a week away.

As soon as the words had exited Right mouth, Satoko gave Hideo a "just as we thought" glance, to which her husband responded with a resigned look. Both continued to sip their soup while Right explained his plan. After a little while, though, unable to take any more, Satoko spoke up in a weary tone: "You know this house it too cold for her. She will likely get sick as soon as she returns."

As anticipated, Right was incensed. *"Damare!"* (Difficult as it was to believe, he was telling his mother to "shut up.")

Hideo openly agreed with his wife, reiterating that bringing Ba-chan back to the house was a bad idea. As soon as the words left Hideo's mouth, Right grabbed his soup bowl and flung the hot contents at his father's face. He then proceeded to flip the table on its side and lunge toward his mother.

Ordinarily I was the target of Right's anger, but this time I was overlooked—free to pull Right from behind.

"Let her go!" I insisted, tugging at his arm.

By this time Right's father had come between his son and his wife.

"Why are you so angry?" Hideo asked; his ability to remain at least ostensibly calm impressed me.

Right was quick to answer: "Because you don't take care of Ba-chan!"

With Right momentarily distracted, Satoko was able to run from the room. Hideo grabbed a towel and began soaking it in running water to cool his face.

My husband was breathing hard, panting like an animal as I coaxed him to retreat from the scene.

"Don't worry," I assured him in a soothing tone. "I will help you with Ba-chan."

Once Right was settled in the north wing, I returned to the kitchen to clean up the mess. As I was wiping the floor, Satoko passed by, carrying a suitcase. Announcing that she was going to her brother's house for a few days, she asked me to take care of the house in her absence.

The next day, instead of heading to the *ryojinhomu*, Right and I visited the local hardware store, where my husband assembled a long list of tools and building supplies, asking to have them delivered as soon as possible. Using these materials and rudimentary building skills, the dutiful grandson turned Ka-chan's sunny sanctuary, the space where she folded laundry and mended clothes, into a western-style bedroom complete with running water and a makeshift tub fashioned from a livestock feeder. Hideo, who observed the strange construction project taking place, transforming what had been a pleasant sitting space into an odd, out-of-place paneled room within a room, dared not say a word.

This was all done before Satoko returned and the seed-sowing monkey appeared on the side of Mt. Kinpoku, signaling that it was time for farmers in the valleys and foothills to begin planting their crops. I saw the monkey one warm spring afternoon as the five of us, Ba-chan included, enjoyed an American-style barbecue in the back garden. It took me a while to see the monkey, but finally I caught on. The snow had melted, exposing a large, continuous patch of bare ground that was indeed shaped like a monkey sitting on its haunches with its hand extended; in the hand there appeared to be a large seed. It made sense that a good farmer might look for the monkey to determine the best day to plant.

Not long after the monkey's shape distorted and the bare spot on the mountain became like any other patch of spring thawed ground, we received a visit from two demons—the same neighborhood dancers I had watched years ago at our local Obon festival the time I had won the tea cups for my rendition of Sado Okesa. Without waiting for an invitation, the creatures slid open our front door, stepped inside, and began to thrash about. I watched from the top of the entryway as the black-haired one whipped his long wig in front of me. These demons, I was told, were good ones who had come to chase away evil.

What? I thought, confused. Hadn't we just chased out the demons with the beans a few weeks earlier? Was this some kind of demon mafia?

As the demons finished their routine, Ka-chan reached into her purse and handed the troupe a small donation. Seemingly satisfied, the pair sauntered off to exorcise the evil from the next house.

That night I experienced a disconcertingly vivid vision. A demon, feeling himself entitled to more than Satoko had given him, pinned me down and raped me in the north wing as my husband lay sleeping on the mat next to mine. It struck me that the whole thing might have been more than a dream; I felt certain I had been completely awake when the incident occurred.

In Japan the school year begins in April, but Right, who was supposed to be studying for a teaching certificate, had done little in the preceding months to prepare for the required exam. Just when I was thinking Right had blown his opportunity to find work as a teacher on Sado, Hideo announced that the girls' high school in town was desperate for a fill-in chemistry and science teacher. If Right were interested, Hideo had connections to make it happen. Teaching wasn't something Right wanted to do, but he took the part-time job for the equivalent of about $1,500 a month.

In his absence I was in charge of Ba-chan. I prepared all of her meals, fed, and changed her. While this kept me occupied for several hours a day, I was glad to be asked by various townspeople whether I could tutor English. This was another outlet.

Right, who disliked teaching, to his credit stuck with it. Once when he took me to his school, I asked whether he conducted lessons in the chemistry lab, to which he answered with a dismissive "No. These girls are too stupid." He went on to explain that on most days he simply wrote on the blackboard and made the students copy his notes.

While caring for Ba-chan I seldom got into trouble with Right. If he had any complaints he targeted his parents for what he considered their waste of time and attention on "unimportant" things like yard work and community involvement. Before my arrival in Sado, Right had bragged about his home, with its expansive garden and temple, and had taken pride in his family's long history. Now I often wondered, *How does Right think Jinzo has survived all these years? Does he think houses, gardens, and graves magically maintain themselves?*

By the time summer rolled around, I had a routine going. When Ba-chan was napping and I had no students to tutor, I would go down the hill to town for groceries and scope out the next book or hair ribbon I wanted to buy. Most of the time I walked, but occasionally, when I was concerned about getting back in a timely manner, I'd take Right's old bicycle.

It was on one of these trips that I experienced a minor bicycle accident. It was nothing serious, but when Right saw that I was skinned from head to toe he took over my care—suddenly becoming an expert in medicine. He was insistent that instead of changing my bandages regularly I should leave the pads as they were originally placed; occasionally dousing them with alcohol until they naturally fell off.

While I was fortunate that my face healed quickly, a large piece of gauze became imbedded in my knee, and although Right had trimmed the lifted edges regularly, the center never released. Having endured numerous surgeries and procedures from my childhood accident, I had known better than to leave the bandage on in the first place, but I had been obedient.

While I was dealing with my grossly infected knee, Ba-chan became lethargic and refused to eat. When we reported her symptoms to the nursing home doctor he directed us to admit her again; his diagnosis was that old woman was suffering from pneumonia and a dietary imbalance.

None of this was surprising, as "Dr. Right" had insisted that his grandmother's room be air conditioned to the degree that even I was often cold, and he had instructed me not to feed his grandmother anything with soy sauce or miso—the primary sources of sodium in the Japanese diet. Right, never acknowledging error, once again took up the cause of rescuing his beloved.

Since Right was teaching, it was up to me to make the daily trek across the valley to the *ryojinhomu* for Ba-chan's feedings. Having only one sighted eye, I found driving the narrow, winding roads harrowing, but somehow I managed each time to make it with many stops and starts. Once again Fujiwara-san and Nakagawa-san were my world from lunchtime through dinner.

In the facility Ba-chan regained strength, to the point that eventually we were able to bring her back to Jinzo with us. Unfortunately, almost as soon as she returned home, just prior to her eighty-eighth birthday—that coveted age that when written out in Chinese characters represents two Mt. Fujis—Ba-chan passed. We rushed her back to the facility, but it was too late. The nurses who had tended to her for the previous three years became her morticians, and following a simple bedside embalming her body was placed in the backseat of our Honda Civic for us to drive home.

Back at Jinzo Right placed the corpse in the makeshift room he had built and turned the air conditioner on high. While Right wandered aimlessly around the house and property, his parents upped the momentum, efficiently making all kinds of arrangements they had evidently rehearsed.

Three priests were hired; catering arranged; and gift sets, each consisting of gourmet bean cakes, grocery store gift certificates, and hand towels, were ordered for each expected guest. The main part of the house was transformed from six separate rooms into one by removing several sets of paper doors, and fresh tatami mats were brought in to replace the existing ones. When the wooden casket arrived, Right carefully laid his ba-chan within, ensuring that she appeared comfortable. Noticing that blood speckles had surfaced around her mouth, he went to town to procure the perfect shade of lipstick, which he painstakingly applied to his grandmother's lips.

Over the next few days, gaudy plastic flower arrangements on easels were delivered and scattered around the garden in front of the main entrance. Neighbors and relatives filled the home as the priest performed various rituals, which included evening prayer vigils involving small drums and hypnotic Buddhist chanting. Right all but ignored the proceedings. There was no talk about his grandmother being in a "happier place" or, for that matter, existing anywhere but in her lifeless state in a box in the room that had by this point been transformed into a tiny freezer.

On the day of the funeral, the house was packed, with all three priests praying at once. Following a large meal, members of the immediate family, along with Ba-chan's casket, were shuttled to the other side of the island by microbus. Upon our arrival at the crematorium, a man with a humped back pushed a stone gurney out to the back of the bus.

I was expecting to receive Ba-chan's remains in a lovely urn, but after spending an hour or so drinking and snacking before a crackling fire we were guided back outside, where the stone gurney awaited us. As we gazed at what little remained of the tough little lady who had kept Jinzo running smoothly through a devastating war and various family struggles, an attendant handed each of us a pair of what appeared to be oversized wooden chopsticks.

Taking the lead, To-chan, followed by his younger brother and sister, began picking through the remains, each selecting bone fragments and placing them into a small box. Everyone else followed, digging around in the macabre pile until nothing remained except ashes to sweep away. I could only imagine that with all the chants and prayers uttered on her behalf, Ba-chan would eventually make it to the place where all good Japanese souls go. For the time being, however, her remains would be staged in the dining room near the prayer altar underneath her large black-and-white portrait until the time of burial several months later.

Ba-chan's passing coincided with the season for worshiping the dead, shortly before the rice harvest. All around Sado, wherever one looked, large bamboo poles were being laced horizontally across trees or other poles; soon these were covered with bunches of rice stalks hanging upside down to dry in the autumn sun.

This year when performing her annual harvest chores, Satoko's steps were noticeably lighter. After thirty or more years of functioning as the *yomesan* (the bride of the house, as opposed to the matriarch), she had finally become queen of her castle. Hideo too was in a better mood, quite possibly a side effect of his wife's more cheerful disposition. It was not that Ba-chan had been forgotten. Both prayed daily for the recently departed, as well as for those who had gone before her. I frequently rose to the smell of incense and the sound of quiet chanting.

While the rest of the house prayed and moved forward, Right seemed to go through only the perfunctory functions of living—for all intents and purposes a man without purpose. The power he had wielded over his parents appeared to have diminished with the old woman's departure. Hideo took over the little room Right had built, using it as a warm place in which to do his paperwork and change his clothes.

Caring for Ba-chan had for months been my primary duty, so the matriarch's loss naturally created a void. I filled my time with tutoring, studying, and general tidying up. Right frequently came home for lunch, and when he did I made him dishes he'd taught me or tried my hand at new recipes I'd learned through Japan's public TV cooking show *"Kyou no Ryori"* ("Today's Dish"). In this manner I made it through my first fall before we headed into our second winter at Jinzo.

There were days when I became a bit bored and had to invent something to do. It was on such a cold, wet day in late January that I decided it was time to do some extensive reorganization of our space. The futon closets had been only partially emptied for our use, and I was forever pushing and shoving around the stacks of old bedding trying to find room. After struggling with the arrangement for so many months, I thought it would be a good idea to pull everything out and start over.

One by one I pulled out the old sleeping mats kept for infrequent guests and stacked them in the middle of the room. As I neared the bottom of the pile, I discovered between the layers something I hadn't expected: four books, three of which were of the same genre, all titled *Petit Tomato*. The fourth was quite different.

Each of the tomato books constituted of a collection of photos featuring one or two girls. Many were Japanese or Asian; others were of unclear ethnicity. Almost all the pictures were nudes, either partial or complete, and all featured natural outdoor backgrounds. I estimated the ages of the models to be somewhere between eight and thirteen, with the average approximately ten. In some of the partially nude photos, the girls were wearing school uniforms with nothing underneath; in their squatting positions one could catch a glimpse of their private areas.

The fourth book featured adult Japanese women. Rather than having been photographed where the sunlight could have enhanced the beauty of their olive skin, all appeared in dark hotel rooms serving as makeshift studios. Around their necks were collars and chains, and their bodies were smeared in feces. In some photos men stood over the women, pissing on them.

Utterly furious, I couldn't begin to absorb the enormity of the situation. As I sat stone still holding the books, I noticed a tag indicating that a couple of them had been purchased at a large department store in Niigata City. This meant that this caliber of material was readily available to anyone—for sale on the open market. *Weren't there laws prohibiting the sale of pornography?*

Confused and profoundly disturbed, my overriding impulse was to take the pile out to the trash and light a fire, but better judgment prevailed. Gathering up the offending material, I went to look for Satoko. My mother-in-law had often privately confessed to me her troubles regarding her son, but I had rarely, if ever, initiated a complaint about Right to her. Now I needed some clarity.

I found her sitting in the *chanoma* watching a late-morning talk show while folding laundry. Kneeling wordlessly next to her, I spread out the collection on the floor.

"Right was hiding these between the futons," I explained simply, watching for her reaction.

Right's mother peered over the lenses of her glasses. "*Maaa!*" was her initial response—the Japanese equivalent to a rolling of the eyes, accompanied by "*Jeeze!*" She followed this up with a simple "I don't know why he spends money this way. He has bought so many of these since he was a teenager, using our money."

This was hardly the response I had expected. I picked up one of the books and flipped through the pages to give Satoko a better sense of the real issue.

"The pictures...these are all of children!" I felt somehow foolish having to spell out my concern.

This sometimes inscrutable woman—the same one who had appeared to be on my side when it came to Right's "selfishness," as she described it—not only didn't appear disgusted but seemed not to so much as flinch. She was in my opinion hardly holding up her end of the sisterhood she had attempted to establish when she had cried on my shoulder about Right, complaining of his self-centered nature and of how poorly he treated her. I reverted—by necessity, it seemed—to being completely blunt.

"Aren't these books banned by law?" I asked.

Satoko was an educated woman who had taught grade school children... little girls like the ones in the pictures. I had expected her to be as incensed as I was.

Mother put down her work and looked for the first time directly at me. "Men are terrible things, aren't they?"

Men? You mean to tell me this is normal? I thought.

Satoko offered little support to my cause so I left her and returned to our room where I carefully replaced the books exactly as I had found them and continued with my cleaning, fuming all the while. There was no way I was going to *ganman* (persevere)…no way in hell I was going to allow such material—or even such thoughts—to share my personal space.

When Right returned home from teaching, I didn't greet him at the door as I usually did but waited for him to find me. As he entered our rooms, I felt suffused by a rush of utter disdain.

Waving my arm in a demonstrative "Vanna White" fashion, I introduced to my husband our freshly cleaned space.

"See, I've found a place for everything. It looks nice, doesn't it?"

I was well aware that my mannerisms were completely out of character—absolutely contrary to what Right had meticulously taught me over the years—and that he would certainly address the matter. His eyes were glaring directly into mine.

"It wasn't easy, you know," I pushed forward, standing up. "I had to move a lot of things around—reorganize, you know."

With this I moved toward the large closet and opened the doors as though to reveal a fabulous prize on the "Price is Right Showcase Showdown." I was completely over the top.

"Like this bedding…I had to take it out and restack it."

Right moved closer.

"Oh, wait a minute. This blanket is a little crooked." I reached underneath and pulled the books forward so they would naturally fall to the floor. Feeling as though I had every reason to cuss, I looked Right squarely in the eyes.

"What in the hell are these?" I asked in a strained voice I barely recognized as my own.

I half expected to be pinned against the wall, but Right didn't flinch. Instead, he nonchalantly replied, "Oh, they are just part of my collection."

The tone of Right's response was somewhere between that of a sheepish child who has been caught being naughty and a man ready to defend what was "rightfully" his.

"This is *child pornography!*" I pointed out—unnecessarily, the way I saw it.

To my surprise Right disagreed, pointing out that he could buy the magazines anywhere and that this was considered a form of art. "In fact," he threw in, as though the input would help me see the light, "these pictures were taken by a woman."

"I don't care who took them," I replied through gritted teeth. "Men use these books for their pleasure, and it's immoral!"

To this Right replied that when boys first become interested in the opposite sex they're only twelve or so. At that age they're looking at the girls around them—girls of the same age, girls they can't have. It was only natural, he pointed out in what struck me as the most bizarre possible extension of logic, for boys to carry with them throughout their teenaged years and into adulthood the fantasy of the girls they couldn't touch. "Such photos are a beautiful memory."

I argued for another ten minutes or so, straining to wring out every last incontrovertible, nuanced drop of the logic I'd gleaned from my classes, but Right would neither allow me to touch his books nor agree to throw them out.

"You cannot judge the world by your values," Right maintained. "Who says we are wrong for thinking these books contain art?"

"Only the majority of the world" was my rueful answer, but Right didn't think my position would win out if the entire population of the planet were polled; my sexually inhibited Judeo-Christian views were definitely in the minority.

Right bent down and picked up his books. "There is nothing bad about looking at a young, perfect body," he disputed. "Nothing at all."

The next day after Right had left for school, I went down the hill to our little town to investigate. There were only a couple of shops I frequented besides the grocery store, one of which sold comics. Right had introduced me to the Arale Norimaki series, and every couple of weeks I would stop in for a new issue. The tale of the little robot girl was entertaining, and reading it constituted a part of my language studies.

The bookstore was small, consisting of only three short aisles, but it carried everything I had needed so far. I searched for the tomato books but didn't find any on display. Relieved, I decided to pick up another sixth-grade-level title for myself.

As I thumbed through selections aimed at preteens, I noticed a young man wearing the uniform of the agriculture high school in the next town. He must have been skipping class. Surreptitiously I watched as he engaged in *tachiyomi* ("stand reading"), something I tried not to do in the local shop because I thought it rude.

The young man appeared most interested in the popular men's weeklies, thick comic magazines sold everywhere. Having picked up a copy once at a train station kiosk and thumbed through it, I distinctly remembered seeing some questionable images among the scenes—drawings of schoolgirls in provocative poses, their underwear peeking out, as though accidently, from beneath their skirts. There were even blurred or muted depictions of their private parts. *Was this really commonplace, or was it by chance I'd selected the only risqué comic on the stand?*

After the student walked away, I went over and looked at the array of magazines. As my eyes took in the colorful and busy cover art, I took special note of the female characters, every one of whom appeared to be young and wearing a skirt—a school uniform much shorter than actually allowed. Instead of purchasing my usual sweet story, I selected one of the men's periodicals for my afternoon reading.

As I exited with my purchase, I realized it was just after noon. A group of girls from the high school down the street—the one at which Right taught—strode briskly past the storefront in a tight pack, laughing together about something.

Observing them from behind, I began to imagine how it must feel for Right to stand day after day in front of them, to take in thirty or forty fresh young faces looking up at him as their authority figure. Then I wondered how it was for the girls to sit in front of a man who more than likely enjoyed undressing them with his eyes. Whether or not they intuited Right's preferences, they had to be at least subconsciously aware of their general objectification in society.

Once home I holed up with my chosen read, starting from the beginning. Every now and then, situated as though at random between pages of story line and intrigue, there appeared female characters, depicted as being much younger than my own twenty-three years, innocently exploring their burgeoning sexuality as young teens are prone to do.

Much of what was portrayed was natural preteen behavior, but some scenes were uncompromisingly vulgar—drawn for the voyeuristic pleasure of men. In all cases the private parts, both male and female, were poorly disguised, though in some fashion blurred or muted. In some cases vaginas were depicted as voids or black holes. It seemed as though the magazine's creator thought schoolgirl vaginas were mysterious galaxies into which lucky rocket ships traveled to experience the Milky Way.

A jumble of sensations churned in my mind as I digested what amounted to daily reading for many Japanese men. I was having a hard time reconciling the values with which I'd grown up with things I had seen and heard during my time in Japan and then, in turn, with Right's actions and words. *One thing I knew: I'd never accept this aspect of Japan.*

I must somehow have compartmentalized all of this, though, because my life did go on without interruption. But even as I stayed on Sado in the house of Jinzo, something within me had changed. Although I already dressed, spoke, and acted younger than my years, somehow I got the idea that I wanted to be smaller. Because I was so tall, people often used *dekai*, or "large," to describe me, and although this was uttered in reference to my height I disliked the word. Little by little I reduced my caloric intake in an effort to shrink myself down to a more acceptable size.

By the time the seed-sowing monkey appeared once again I weighed just 115 pounds, and *dekai* had been replaced by *hosoi*, or "thin," as the most common adjective used to describe me. In America people had always called me "skinny," but in Japan I hadn't to this point been able to squeeze into a medium, which seemed to be the only available size when it came to cute clothes. After eating a diet that primarily consisted of fermented beans and Sado seaweed jelly, I was finally able to wear almost anything off the rack.

Right never mentioned the change in my appearance—perhaps he simply didn't notice. Something was going on with him, and shortly after the monkey had melted into the mountainside I learned that he had been contemplating another move. Sentiments he had voiced over the phone while still in Michigan resurfaced; he saw no reason to live on in Japan without the grandmother who had raised him. And that was that.

Nothing I said could dissuade Right. He didn't like teaching, and there were no other jobs that suited him on Sado. While he could undoubtedly have found work on the main island, he had no desire to do so, citing the higher cost of living. When I asked about Jinzo and the legacy, Right replied rather evasively that maybe someday when he retired from work we would return here to live. Even if Right were to follow through with his long-term plan, his parents would be over ninety...if they were still alive.

While most Japanese parents would have been disappointed at the news that the child who was supposed to care for them in their old age was going to live abroad, there was no protest whatsoever from Hideo and Satoko. My guess was that they had given up hope that their son would become respectful and fulfill his duties. In their minds it was preferable to experience thirty years of peace, followed by a handful in a nursing home, than to live with an egocentric, ill-tempered son.

Before spring was over, I had once again packed our things into sturdy tangerine boxes and sent them back across the ocean. Within the sixteen or so boxes were several binders of nude photos my husband had carefully selected as the best of his collection, along with a couple dozen laser discs—video recordings for which we didn't even own a player. The discs, which were quite expensive, had appeared—at least to my knowledge—out of nowhere. Among them were classic samurai movies, car-racing videos, and some newer Japanese animated movies.

Right led me to believe that I would experience summers in Japan, so I left my tulip *yukata*, hoping for an occasional Obon dance. But for now I would have to settle for the same Japanese life I'd led prior to our move to Sado—for my Japan away from Japan. I found myself far from what I'd wished for when I'd so long ago put my little temple doll, the *daruma*, into play.

CHAPTER 9

Auto Wife

The seed-sowing monkey followed us back to Michigan. I was pregnant, and with this news a new chapter in my bonsai *life had begun. This was something I'd always wanted—to give birth to a beautiful Japanese baby and raise him or her firmly within the culture. But I had concerns. First, I would most assuredly become matronly in Right's eyes—a prematurely old woman. Second, with a child there would be more tasks and hence more opportunities for error. At the top of my worry list was the fear of having a little girl. How would I protect her as she grew from all of the ogling eyes?*

I ACTUALLY LEARNED OF MY pregnancy within weeks of returning to Michigan. This was joyous news, but I couldn't imagine how Right would function as a father and suspected his treatment of me might change for the worse. While it was already difficult for me to manage everything that might set him off, I knew I would have to be more disciplined than ever.

For the first time in his life, at twenty-eight years old, Right secured a real job: engineering work with a Japanese automotive parts manufacturer in the center of the state, an hour from where I had grown up. With funds provided by his parents, we purchased a new car, rented an apartment, and set it up with brand new furnishings, including the accoutrements for a nursery.

As always, I took pride in being a dutiful Japanese wife. Every morning I laid out Right's pressed work clothes so he wouldn't have to waste time selecting them. I wiped and polished his shoes, always making sure they were pointed toward the door so he could slip them on in one fluid motion and go. I prepared for him five-course lunches that included soup, rice, and three types of side dishes. Meal choices were not to be repeated during the course of any given month, so I kept a calendar rotation of Right's favorites. On many days, Right would boast, his warm Japanese bento box was the best furnished at his lunch table. I didn't doubt him.

I did my best to minimize the negative effects the pregnancy would have on my body, while still doing my best for my baby. I exercised to Jane Fonda's pregnancy workout video and consumed as much protein as I could. Since I couldn't find any cute maternity dresses that matched the style I'd adopted in Japan, I created patterns out of newspaper and sewed my own from scratch. When the baby had sufficiently developed inside me, I began a daily routine of reading Japanese fairy tales aloud to my unborn child.

While I looked forward to being a mother, my fears, rational or otherwise, would often get the better of me. Oprah failed to help. Her interviews with victims of this or that abuse only fueled my insecurities. A local news story about twin baby girls having been molested practically sent me over the edge.

I had let the "Petit Tomato" topic go, stuffing it down in my subconscious for several months, but one evening I found myself compelled to ask Right for reassurance. I asked him how Japanese men could look at young girls as objects of desire and still refrain from acting upon such feelings.

His answer was that such thoughts were fantasy based—*"completely outside of reality."* In fact, he added, acting upon such fiction essentially ruins the fantasy aspect forever. Besides, Japanese fathers are often so close with their daughters that they take baths with the little girls right up until puberty, when the girls themselves naturally pull away. It was much the same for mothers and sons. This closeness wasn't sexual in any way—more like a close, protective bond. He would never think of damaging the relationship by mixing fantasy with reality.

This explanation was not at all satisfying; I couldn't fathom how one could entertain a fantasy—itself a type of desire—while maintaining the self-control never to act upon it. In any case I wasn't in a position to argue.

Although I had hoped for a boy during this year of the rabbit, we had a little girl. Right thought this was perfect; if we were to have a boy second, our little girl would at a young age learn how to mother. Evidently this was the common thought among Japanese, even though I, growing up American, had always thought an older brother protector was the ideal situation.

Our baby was given a common Japanese first name with Chinese characters that stood for "gorgeous lake"—a Michigan reference. For her middle name Right insisted upon his grandmother's. Right immediately directed his parents to complete the family register by adding "Gorgeous" to the town record as a member of Jinzo.

With the birth of my precious daughter, I could no longer feign being a young girl myself. I was a mother, responsible for a strikingly beautiful child, so full of promise. To this end we requested from Right's parents regular shipments of board books, toys, clothing, and video tapes of children's shows.

Entering our apartment was like visiting Japan in microcosm. We had everything a Japanese child living in Tokyo might have. By the time Gorgeous turned one, I had memorized 150 Japanese children's songs and dozens of fairy tales. As I raised my daughter, I in effect raised myself; having learned Japanese from an adult perspective, I was now relearning the language from baby talk on up.

As Gorgeous grew it became clear that she was a determined child. Before she could talk she was constructing tall towers and piecing together complex puzzles. Her success was mine. She would not, I was determined, be uneducated or behind—nor would she be under the thumb of any man. While Right worked—he was to my surprise and satisfaction becoming quite the company man—my baby and I summered on Sado Island, where onlookers commonly exclaimed that Gorgeous looked like a doll. I relished the attention paid her; having felt myself to be an ugly child, I took vicarious pride in her beauty.

It was just after Gorgeous's second birthday that I became pregnant again. In perfect Japanese birth order—girl first, boy second—we completed our family with a boy whom, for obvious reasons, we named Great Lake. For a middle name Right had chosen that of a mythological Japanese hero. Strange as this may seem Right believed that, should someone learn his "true identity," our son could wind up the target of some murderous plot.

Not long after Great's birth in 1991, Right became restless with what he viewed to be his low pay and long hours, so we moved from a relatively small town to Detroit's downriver area, where my aspiring husband took a job as a design engineer in Mazda's new plant. There we found a large transplant community of Japanese families supporting the company's joint venture with Ford; instantly we were accepted.

The timing couldn't have been more ideal. Although we spoke only Japanese at home and offered all the trappings provided by Right's parents, Right and I were in agreement that Gorgeous and Great spent entirely too much time alone with me as their teacher. Clearly they needed exposure to other children like themselves in order to fully realize their cultural identity. Within a few weeks we were invited to join two mother-child clubs, the Donguri Club (Chestnut Club), exclusively for the wives of Mazda men, and the Kyabetsu Club (Cabbage Club), which extended its membership to any Japanese wife, regardless of her husband's company of employment.

Both clubs were impeccably organized. There were subteams of mothers within each club who rotated educational entertainment, snack duties, and newsletter duties. In addition to regular meetings, there were various informal teas and play dates. This was an elaborate social network intended to support the wives and children of men who had been shipped here to head up both the big plant and the supporting suppliers.

In terms of young family life in Japan, I had witnessed very few examples. I had learned how to be a housewife during my time on Sado, but I hadn't been exposed to young Japanese mothers for any length of time. In the clubs I was able to observe not only how the mothers spoke to their children but also how they reprimanded them.

Even though the company wives were living in the United States, they took pride in dressing their children in Japanese clothes and feeding them Japanese snacks purchased from exclusive shops in the northern suburbs. The children all played with the latest toys from Japan; I was careful to take note of anything we might have been missing and to ask Right's parents to send equal or better. Gorgeous was in possession of a magical Sailor Moon wand that afforded her super strength, along with a Rika-chan doll collection (the Japanese equivalent to Barbies) that rivaled that of any full-blooded Japanese girl in our circles. Great had no lack of monsters and weapons from several "ranger" series, including Jyuu-ranger and Dai-ranger—the precursors of the wildly popular Power Ranger show that would eventually debut in the United States.

While I was busily raising our children in the Japanese way, Right was becoming a good "salary man." Japanese housewives have a saying that a good husband works late and brings home the sushi, and I subscribed to this philosophy wholeheartedly. In fact, I liked to have Right arrive home as late as possible. Although my husband's work ethic had dramatically improved since our time on Sado, nothing else about him had changed. In fact, based on the complexities children naturally bring with them, I was required to expend a good deal more energy keeping Right's temper at bay. I was careful to get as much as possible accomplished while he was at work and, whenever possible, even to put the children to bed before he returned from his hard day.

It was abundantly clear to me that as a *ka-chan* (mama) I had become somewhat disgusting to Right. At twenty-nine I was older than any female in Right's collection of photo books, and I had a recurring nightmare about my teeth falling out. According to a book I read about dream interpretation, this is a telltale sign that I feared growing old.

Right would regularly stare me down with utter disdain based on the most trivial household error. Even after I had mitigated his anger somewhat by quickly apologizing, it was never enough. Several nights a week he would sleep in a chair in the TV room after watching porno flicks. I had come to loathe both him and the way he treated me.

Every morning as I saw Right off to work, I managed to close the door carefully, so as not to make a sound, just as he'd taught me (*closing doors or drawers or even setting things down with too much force is considered improper*). And as soon as I had completed this action, I would utter "I hate you!" under my breath. This was an uncontrollable response, a reflex reaction to feeling forced to hold onto so much internal anger and tension. Had Right been American I'm reasonably certain I would have left him long before, but being a Japanese wife and living in the culture had become my identity for all intents and purposes, replacing everything I'd known before—which had been precious little, given my insular background and young age at the time of leaving it. Without Right all of that would disappear. So I resolutely made the choice to *ganman*—to persevere through and stay the course.

By this time, almost twelve years into my transformation, I could no longer distinguish "myself" at all. On the inside I screamed as though something ominous were crawling beneath my skin. There were times when, driving down the highway, I visualized putting the pedal to the floor and ending everything in a fiery crash. I often worried that I would go suddenly insane while carrying Great and accidentally drop him on the concrete. For fear of compulsively stabbing myself in the stomach, I was careful never to keep a knife within sight on the kitchen counter.

I was in this state of mind when an article in the *Detroit Free Press* about the University of Michigan's Dearborn campus induced me to consider finishing my degree—the one I had started prior to our move to Sado years earlier. During our second year of marriage, I had nearly lost my mind, but when I had applied myself to formal studies my confidence had improved, and my situation and outlook had changed for the better. Maybe, just maybe, schooling would again now be the cure. Unaware of my precarious psychological state, Right agreed to the plan on the grounds that I would view this course of action as being educated for the children's sake.

When I started my classes at the university, Gorgeous had just begun attending weekend Japanese school in the northern suburbs. Mine was a tough balancing act, considering the complexities of our home life, but I was determined to manage everything without missing a beat. For the most part I did, but whenever

I slipped up Right's criticisms of my intelligence and ability stung all the more. My husband's critiques simply didn't match the affirmation I was constantly receiving from my professors. How long could I bring myself to say "I'm sorry" for niggling issues that didn't matter or for crimes I hadn't committed? After my having racked up a couple semesters of straight As, the inevitable happened.

It had been a long time since I had challenged Right about anything, but one night I flipped. At the dinner table in front of the children Right accused me, as he regularly did, of something I had in no way done. Electing not to apologize for the apparent indiscretion, I kept eating. When he forcefully accused me a second time, I flat out informed him that he was wrong.

"I'm sorry," I said rather perfunctorily, "but I didn't do that which you speak of."

Right was in shock. "*What* did you say?"

I repeated myself, to which he issued a stern warning—really a veiled threat. "You better watch yourself!"

Unable to stand for my indignation any longer, Right grabbed his large, frosted mug of beer and flung it over Great's head, smashing it against the living room fireplace. He then proceeded to systematically shatter our plates and rice bowls against the dining room wall. That completed, he trudged upstairs.

Gorgeous was sobbing, and Great's eyes were wide as the three of us wordlessly surveyed the destruction. Food was stuck to the walls, and the fine china shards I had become accustomed to sweeping up were everywhere. In that moment I felt terribly guilty. All it would have taken was the customary "I'm sorry. Yes, I understand."

One by one I picked up my babies, carried them across the minefield to the *chanoma* room, and gated them in. Then I got down on my hands and knees and began gathering the tiny pieces of glass that seemed to have flown everywhere. After two hours of cleaning I went upstairs to beg Right's forgiveness.

If I wanted to continue in school, I realized, I had to accept the dichotomy of my existence. For a few hours in class each day I could hold my chin up, be whoever I wanted to be, but at home I had to shut off that part of myself in deference to Right.

As I continued racking up As, I set my sights on winning several academic awards. To facilitate this I had begun interjecting some shortcuts into my routines. This had resulted in a gradual shift in my level of care—so gradual as to be almost imperceptible. To me, that is.

It had begun with simple things. Instead of washing the potatoes thoroughly both before and after peeling them, I simply peeled and used them as they were. If no one were around I would do forbidden things, such as using a counter rag to quickly wipe up a floor spill. When the children played, I often let them go a little longer than usual without checking on them. I assumed that what Right didn't see he wouldn't know, but one day it all caught up with me.

It was a sunny Sunday afternoon in May, and the children wanted to go to the local schoolyard and play. Right was occupied, relaxing in the *chanoma* watching TV, so it fell to me to take them. I was in the midst of studying for finals, but the kids were being noisy, so it was just as well that I take them. By way of compromise I grabbed my texts and headed with them out the door.

Both Gorgeous and Great loved slides, and as soon as we arrived at the park they headed straight to the yellow curly one. I watched them closely for a time as they happily and repeatedly clambered up and slid back down, racing and chasing each other in between. After standing nearby for a while, I took a seat a dozen or so yards away and began to review my notes.

Dividing my attention, I simultaneously studied and watched the children play. All was well until I heard Great screaming in panic.

"*Inu! Inu!*" he was screeching, indicating that there was a dog somewhere in the vicinity. Great was completely frozen at the top of the tallest slide. Right had taught the children that dogs were dirty and dangerous, and both were extremely afraid of them.

Instantaneously predicting what was about to happen, I jumped up from the bench and darted to the slide. But before I could reach the children, little Great had lost his footing and fallen through his sister's arms.

I heard the ominous thud as his head hit the concrete below; it sounded like a pumpkin.

Looking around for help I saw no one, so I picked up my screaming boy and cradled his body horizontally. His eyes were rolled back, and he had begun to convulse. I began walking at a fast pace, still steady enough to avoid jostling my inert son.

I sent Gorgeous ahead to alert her father to call 911. It took every bit of strength I had to carry my nearly four-year-old the three blocks back to our house.

By the time I reached the front door, Great had calmed down. As I went to open the door I found Right on the other side, simply waiting.

Glaring at me, Right took Gorgeous's hand and proceeded without a word to the TV room, leaving me alone with our son. No sooner did he shut the door than Great began to scream and vomit.

I called out, "We need to call nine one one!"

Right appeared in the doorway. "You take care of it! It's *your* problem!"

Within minutes the ambulance and a police car had arrived. Great screamed and fought as he was being strapped to the gurney. Right came out once to see what was going on. After a perfunctory glance, and saying nothing, he retreated back into his sanctuary.

Great and I spent the next couple of hours at our small local hospital before being referred to the children's hospital downtown. The doctor had discovered what appeared to be a hairline crack in his skull and thought it best that we go by ambulance and be seen by a specialist.

As we waited to be transported I called Right. I had barely gotten the diagnosis out of my mouth before he began hurling accusations.

"Do you know what I found out? *Do you? Huh?*" His voice was rising, both in pitch and decibel level.

I knew precisely what he was going to say: I had been neglectful in my duties. I should have been standing underneath the slide, arms extended at the ready.

"I went back to the school with Gorgeous, and she showed me exactly what happened! You were not watching!"

Tears rolled down my cheeks as Right continued to describe in great detail, based on the information he had gleaned from our daughter, what had occurred and then to cast blame squarely on me for being negligent—as though the guilt were not already tearing me up.

After being admitted to the children's hospital and undergoing a second regimen of poking and prodding, Great was finally permitted to fall asleep. As I sat in the windowsill watching his chest move up and down, I replayed the whole scene in slow motion in my head: Great's scream. The menacing dog in the corner of the playground. Great slipping through his sister's arms. I could hear the thud, the awful sound.

I sobbed as I looked out over the hospital parking lot. Even though everyone was assuring me that Great would be fine, I was fairly certain *I* would never be. Right was going to shove that day in my face—smearing it like the feces on the faces of those women in the book I had discovered among the sleeping mats—over and over again for the rest of my life. From this point on anything our son would struggle in doing would be attributed to the fall and to my neglect.

After all of this I still had the notes for my aesthetics text in hand. Gorgeous had carried them home for me when she had run to summon her father. I opened the book and tried to read, but the words only blurred. Unable to see through my tears, I closed the book and held it tightly against my chest.

The next day, as the still hospitalized Great and I played a windup fishing game I had found at the hospital gift shop, an entourage of five white coats showed up at our door. Among them was a large black woman. She stepped forward, introduced herself as Dr. Canady, and went over to Great's bed.

"You like fishin'?" she asked him, leaning over the railing.

My son, probably scared of being poked again, didn't reply. I myself could barely speak. The arrival of the medical team had caused me to start crying again, and I had to catch my breath in preparation for saying anything.

"He really only speaks Japanese," I explained, sucking back air.

The doctor looked me up and down. "Well, miss, you don't look Japanese to me!"

I explained our situation, after which Dr. Canady proceeded to pull out a flashlight and check the dilation in Great's pupils, along with his overall level of responsiveness.

"Ma'am, I've looked at his x-rays. You don't have nothin' to worry about."

I looked down, shaking my head almost reflexively from side to side.

"Listen to me." Dr. Canady's voice was firm and steady. "He's going to be all right. You, on the other hand, are a mess!" With that she wrapped her thick arms around me and gave me a squeeze. I fell completely apart.

"You don't understand," I objected between gasps. "It's my fault, and my husband knows it!"

"He's a strong boy! You didn't think he would fall now, did you? This was an accident, girl, and you gotta get that through your head!"

After hearing that my husband was blaming me for what had happened, Dr. Canady offered to call Right and straighten out the situation. Emphatically I pleaded with her: this would do no good; calling him would only cause more trouble for me.

After the doctor had gone, I considered what she'd said regarding Great's fall having been an accident. "Accident" was a word Right never used. To him nearly any exigency was preventable. To that day Right blamed my parents for my own long-ago accident. After all, he reasoned, if they hadn't let me ride my bike after dinner on that fateful day in 1969 I would have grown up with two functional eyes. A particularly poignant accusation from my point of view was the one regarding one of his aunts and her mentally challenged son. Right insisted that if his aunt hadn't kept her baby so long in her womb, his cousin—the one no one cared to talk about—would have been born normal.

In my husband's opinion the negative result of any situation with human involvement could be traced back to lack of intelligence and forethought—to a screw-up of some kind. Right may have seemed overly staunch about this point, but it was the Japanese way to accept fault and minimize or avoid excuses. The compassion and forgiveness with which I'd grown up were for the weak-minded.

While I could accept responsibility for what had happened, this didn't negate the fact that there was something horribly wrong with Right's behavior. There had always been something wrong, but somehow, for the sake of that all-important culture I'd dealt with it. Much as Ba-chan had been Right's leverage over Satoko, the children were Right's leverage over me. It was all about control.

I'd danced with demons long enough.

CHAPTER 10

Yesterday Once More

The first step to recovery is admitting you are an addict, but at this point I didn't even realize I had a problem. There were no rehab centers for cultural addiction...no specialists...no detox. At the time I assumed Right was my issue; if I could just replace him I'd be fine. I longed for the Japan I'd first encountered—the one filled with moon rabbits.

GREAT SEEMED NONE THE WORSE for wear as soon as he was back in familiar surroundings, but despite this and Dr. Canady's clearance Right was sure Great had sustained some level of damage. Since Right would not allow our son to attend his preschool, I received permission from my professors to bring him along to my exams which I took in their offices.

After the accident I could have gone on doing what I had always done—acquiescing to whatever bogus accusation was being thrown my way, accepting every ounce of blame for any noticeable blip in Great's development—but that fall from the slide had been the beginning of the end. Seeds of rebellion had been planted with Right's reaction to my pleas for help for our son.

It had been my plan to spend the summer on Sado with the children as soon as Gorgeous finished her Japanese Saturday school classes in late June.

We had tickets, but after the fall Right put these plans on hold to enable him to observe how Great would do. Right had purchased a boxing helmet for our son to wear at all times, and I was to follow behind him everywhere to keep him from running about. Being that Great was a particularly *kappatsu* (active) child, this was no easy task. While the seeds of rebellion were germinating, I followed Right in this regard, hoping he might still approve of our scheduled trip. After seeing for himself that Great was perfectly fine, Right at length did allow us to prepare for the trip.

I had not forgotten *his* address—not after at least a hundred letters. With Great in tow I walked into a local telegram office and wrote it in clear block letters across a FedEx envelope. Inside I placed a simple note: "CALL THE TOURIST HOTEL IN UENO ON JULY 7 at 7:00 p.m." I signed it with my last name only—a name by which he wouldn't have known me.

Believing that the message would somehow reach the addressee and trusting that the instructions would be followed, I passed the days leading up to the trip in an almost feverish anticipation. I bought several new short skirts and on a whim a gold ankle bracelet, all of which I hid. While Right was at work, I danced over and over again to George Michael's "Freedom." It was thrilling to harbor a little secret Right could never have imagined. I was ready for a bit of *kibuntenkan*—a change of pace, a renewal of spirit.

Three weeks after I set my plan into motion, the children and I disembarked at Narita Airport. Inside I felt anxious. Timing was everything. We had to catch a train into the city, check in, go out and get some dinner, and bathe—all before 6:30 p.m. My goal was to have the children sound asleep by the magical hour for the 7:00 p.m. call I was expecting. The timing was tight, but the children were good sleepers, and I had deliberately kept them awake and entertained through most of the flight, to the hardly veiled dismay of some of those seated close by.

I had no indication that Yasu would call, but I thought he would. Nervously I watched the clock, and at the appointed hour the phone did predictably ring. It was the front desk, calling to advise me that I had a call from a Kawamura-san.

"*Moshi Moshi,*" I said as the call transferred in.

On the other end: "*Hai. Moshi Moshi. Kawamura desu kedo*" ("Yes. Hello, Hello. This is [Mr.] Kawamura.").

I took a deep breath. His voice hadn't changed. In Japanese I asked whether he knew who I was, to which he replied that he most certainly did. He had called knowing it was me. I breathed a sigh of relief.

To cover an awkward pause—I had no idea what to say next—Yasu spoke up again, asking the most obvious question: "Are you well?"

How could I explain? I answered that I was not doing very well. He asked why…(leaving the end of the thought open ended).

"Oh," I paused. "It's nothing."

Suddenly a flood of memories overwhelmed me. I remembered Yasu and myself together at Mt. Kurohime camp. How many times during those few days together hadn't I faced the fact that we would have to separate, and in those sad moments he had asked me "What's wrong?" and I had replied "Oh…nothing" or something similar?

I suspected that Yasu wasn't calling from home and asked where he was in that moment. Yasu answered that he was calling from his office. I had calculated this exact timing into my plan, knowing that most Japanese men work until at least 7:00 p.m.

"Stacy?"

"*Hai*" (Yes).

"Where is your husband?"

I was happy to tell him he was nowhere around. "He's in America. I am here alone…with my two children. They are sleeping now."

"*Ah! Lucky!* You have children!"

I told him I had a girl and a boy and briefly described them. Yasu expressed envy over my situation and was quick to calculate just how old I had been when I had given birth to each; he recalled the exact date of my birthday.

"Yasu, do you have children?" I asked.

"No, I'm still a bachelor," he replied, laughing.

I was dumbstruck, having been 100 percent certain he would be married. He had been engaged when I had last spoken to him—was that eleven years ago?

I felt the need to reconfirm. "You didn't get married?"

"Hai" ("Yes," meaning that he didn't). I held the phone away from my mouth for a moment and covered the receiver. "Oh, come on! This is too much!" I half whispered to myself.

I proceeded to ask Yasu about girlfriends, whether or not he had one. He said that this was not the case.

"Stacy…can I see you tonight? In one hour?"

Oh my God! I could hardly believe this was happening.

"Yes…*yes!* My children are sleeping. I can leave my room and meet you in the lobby. I would like to see you very much."

Yasu confirmed the location and informed me that he was on his way.

"Omachistitteorimasu." In formal terms I told him I would be waiting.

As I hung up the phone, a sudden rush of adrenaline shot through my body. Wanting to scream, I resorted to hopping around the room shaking my fists in the air like a whacked-out prizefighter.

After regaining my composure, I realized that there was really no private area in the cramped hotel lobby for Yasu and me to talk. On a whim I ran downstairs and booked the room adjacent to mine, providing instructions for the desk clerk.

I took a long, hot bath before dressing in a plaid jumper skirt I thought was particularly youthful looking. Then, as the designated time drew near, I settled into the spare room. On the table I set a bottle of duty-free Michigan wine and two glasses I had purchased at Detroit Metro on the outside chance something like this might actually happen. At last there was a faint knock on the door.

If my heart had been beating hard when the telephone rang, it was now thrusting like a fist between my ribs. I took a deep breath, counted to five, and opened the door. It had been nearly fourteen years since I'd seen this face.

"This hotel is not easy to find! At first I looked on the other side of the station. I didn't know there were any hotels on this side. Finally I started walking around and asking."

Yasu was breathing hard, as though he'd been running.

"Please sit down," I invited rather formally. "I had to get a room because the lobby was too cramped. My children are in the next room. I wanted to be near in case they wake up."

Yasu studied my face. "You look exactly the same."

I didn't have to be told that this wasn't the case. After everything I'd been through—the years of crying and the almost daily breakdowns—I couldn't possibly look like the girl he had known for so short a time.

"How long has it been?" he asked.

"It's been fourteen years, Yasu. I thought of you so many times. I never forgot about you and our days at Kurohime Camp."

This was no lie. Whenever Right had been angry with me I had prayed that Yasu would feel my heart and somehow rescue me from my helpless torment.

"*Ore mo*" ("Me too"), Yasu agreed. "Those days were *saiko yo!*" ("the best!").

I couldn't resist asking about his engagement, the one I had heard about when his mother had called me that summer so long ago when I had attempted to leave Right.

Yasu explained that it just hadn't worked out and that he had come to think of marriage in general as a cumbersome proposition. I had to agree. My experience with marriage had been horrible.

As we talked I studied the mannerisms of my first love. Every nuance, I suspected, would have to satisfy me for a long time.

"Yasu, you look the same to me," I stated honestly, complimenting him.

He laughed. "No, I got fat! Too much drinking. Drinking is my job."

"What do you do?" I asked.

"I work for a construction company. I drink with clients every day. My doctor said I won't live long at this rate."

I poured the wine, and we sipped companionably as we talked. Every few minutes one of us would exclaim how unbelievable it was to actually be in each other's presence. Finally Yasu asked me where I was going in Japan.

"Sado." I said this calmly, as though it were no big deal, knowing that from a typical Japanese perspective Sado was no ordinary destination.

"*Sadogashima*? Eehhh?" Yasu exclaimed, using Sado's formal name. "I have never been to Sadogashima? Why Sado?"

I hated to taint the conversation with mention of Right, but it was unavoidable. "My husband's parents live on Sado."

Yasu, a master of small talk from what I remembered, knew precisely what to say to ease the tension. "The fish is delicious there, isn't it?"

I answered that I liked Sado's fresh raw squid the most.

The conversation flowed naturally in Japanese as we sipped the cherry wine. I hadn't taken a drink for many years. Good girls didn't drink. Now the wine relaxed me. Yasu relaxed me. He wasn't an uptight person like Right.

"Do you still live with your parents?"

Although I had never seen a picture of his room, I had the whole thing mapped out in my mind from descriptions in his letters.

"Of course! I still have all of your letters in my room!" he replied in a teasing manner.

"Well, either you are a lazy housekeeper or you really like my letters," I responded, thinking he had to be kidding.

"It is true. I never clean, and they are my treasures," he laughed. "I can bring them with me the next time I see you! We can read each one!"

I was hopelessly embarrassed at the prospect of viewing them and urged Yasu to throw them all away.

Yasu then asked whether I was a housewife. I told him that I was, proudly adding that I was also a college student studying philosophy. To this he once again expressed envy at my fortunate circumstances.

"You have a husband and children, and you are a person with a good head. What could be better than that?"

I looked down at my feet, and my lower lip quivered. He should never have complimented me like that, I thought almost furiously. I was with a *horrible* man, and I *didn't* have a good head. This was evident by my choices.

Immediately sensing my profound sadness, Yasu reached over and ran his forefinger over my left knee. I tried to keep myself from shaking.

"Shall we meet again?" Yasu asked.

I hadn't thought that far ahead. How would I arrange it? My trip back through Tokyo was already planned for the same day as our flight out of Narita, so this seemed quite impossible. I told Yasu I didn't know when or how.

"I will give you the number of my private line at home and my work number. Call me anytime, okay? Oh, and one more. Here is my pager number."

Leaving the door open for future encounters, he rose to leave. We had talked for nearly two hours, but it had seemed like only about thirty minutes.

After Yasu's departure all kinds of thoughts flitted, unbidden, through my mind. I had hoped the summer would give me clarity, a clear path forward. I needed to be free from Right but still keep my Japanese lifestyle intact, and I had no clue how to accomplish this. *Was it possible the little daruma from so long ago was going to come through, even after I had abused his powers?*

The summer of 1994 was particularly hot, and our daily routine on Sado was established around the thermometer. In the morning I got the children up early to attend radio exercises at the temple up the hill. After that I'd help Gorgeous with her Japanese Saturday school homework. She had to keep two journals during the summer: one of daily events and another reporting the growth of a morning glory seed she had faithfully planted upon our arrival. This was the standard homework of a Japanese first grader, and Gorgeous was not exempt.

Once the homework was finished, the three of us would head out to the community pool across the valley, where we would stay for several hours. After lunch at around one in the afternoon, the heat would become unbearable, and I'd put the children down for a nap in the coolest room.

I could usually count on their napping for about two hours—long enough for me to take a long walk. It was entirely too hot for exercise, but I was up for the torture. I had a lot to think about and needed time alone.

For these walks I always wore one of the minis I had bought for the trip and listened to my George Michael tape. Every day I logged a good five miles—taking as many different routes as I could find. I made it a point to stop at every temple, shrine, and altar, praying for guidance that never seemed to come. Eventually, when walking wasn't enough, I started to run.

I considered the chance I might suffer a heatstroke and die, but at that point I really didn't care. My preoccupation was completely selfish, but I had no idea what I was going to do once the summer was over. So I kept running and running, despite temperatures over hundred degrees, in conjunction with the island's oppressive tropical humidity. Once during one of these runs, a load of Japanese Defense soldiers coming down from their mountain training camp passed me in an open military truck. As they passed I instantly had a perverse thought: if someone, or even an entire gang of men were to rape me, then perhaps I would be too dirty to live in Right's presence. That would be one way out.

Unable to find sleep from all of the turmoil broiling inside me, I took to sneaking out at night, plumping pillows under my blankets and slipping out sliding doors of the north wing, whereupon I'd leap over the goldfish pond and cut through the back garden. From there I'd take a back road down to the valley and make my way by side streets to the small town.

A couple of times I stepped into obscure pubs and had a drink. Another time I discovered a small festival and joined in the dancing. Like a seasoned professional, I performed Sado's famous dance with everything I had. When I finished I sauntered off without saying a word to anyone. Like a mythical character from a Japanese folk tale, I emerged from the bamboo forest and then simply vanished.

As I had done all along, I hid my troubles from Right's parents. They had heard only positive things from our side and had no clue as to how we actually lived. In their eyes I had been dedicated and diligent, a good young bride and wife to their son. Although I was planning to somehow leave their son—which entailed abandoning Jinzo—I kept my mouth shut. Despite my efforts, however, the burning secret inside me manifested itself in odd behavior that hadn't gone unnoticed.

I walked around the house and yard listening to tunes through my Sony Walkman—and singing out loud, something I'd never done before. I knew too that there was a little skip in my step—perhaps the same skip Satoko had used when Ba-chan had passed and Right could no longer badger his mother about her care. On a daily basis I was aware of sidelong glances from my mother-in-law, but I didn't care.

With everything going on in my head, I desperately needed a friend, but beyond the Mazda wives—acquaintances really—I had none. I had sent Yuki birth announcements when my children were born and faithfully sent her a New Years card every year, but she had never replied. I felt an aching compulsion to talk to my Japanese sister.

I thought that perhaps Yuki might have been offended by Right when she met him years earlier and that she had accordingly decided not to bother me—or that perhaps she was married and busy with her own young family. Knowing Yuki as I did, I suspected she might be juggling a career on top of motherhood, becoming a new breed of Japanese woman, a "supermom" who could handle it all.

Whatever the reason for her silence, I was determined to talk to her. After obtaining a new phone number from Yuki's mother, I decided to call. It took multiple late night and "later night" calls to get through, but eventually my sister answered.

Yuki apologized for not responding to my cards and letters stating rather evasively that she had been busy with work—frequently working until 8:00 p.m. or so. From this I assumed she was still single, but just in case she had found a man who would appreciate her ambitious nature, I dared to ask.

"Oh no! I'm not married," she replied emphatically.

When I asked her why not, Yuki gave the standard answer: she had not found her own "Mr. Right"—not that she had the time to date. Then my sister dropped a bomb. "But I do have a son."

I felt I had to check my hearing. How could she have kept this from me?

"*Really?* A son? How old?" I had to confirm what I thought I'd just heard. Japanese women generally didn't "keep" children conceived out of wedlock; they aborted them.

"He's five now. His name is Nobu."

"What about the father?"

"Oh, I don't know," Yuki responded with a sigh. "I didn't want to marry him." I asked Yuki whether her family was helping her, watching her son while she worked. She replied without elaboration that they did not. Because her parents had wanted her to get an abortion she felt they had essentially negated her son's existence, a reality that disturbed her too much to spend much time with them.

We talked for a good thirty minutes before I disclosed my happy secret: that I'd seen Yasu again.

"Really?" This piqued Yuki's interest, as I'd known it would.

I gave my sister a few titillating details—explaining how I had sent him a cryptic note, hoping he would call, and then describing our exciting encounter.

"It was like traveling back in time, Yuki. It was so exciting!"

When my sister asked what my husband would think of my meeting my old flame, she opened the door to me talking about my plan to leave Right. I told Yuki that I hated my husband too much to stay in the house with him another day.

"Well, maybe Yasu still likes you."

Yuki began to sound like the young girl who years earlier had read the love note over my shoulder and declared Yasu to be completely infatuated with me.

"I think he does, but what Japanese guy marries a woman with children? Especially a *gaijin* like me?"

Yuki insisted that there were in fact such men...well, minus the "gaijin part," based on the simple fact that Caucasian women rarely married Asian men.

"Well, I can't depend on what Yasu will or won't do. I have to leave Right for my own sanity," I told her. "But I'm not opposed to having a little fun, and I enjoy Yasu's company."

At the end of the call, Yuki and I agreed to meet on my way out of Japan. This became my excuse to depart Sado a little early. I had secretly rung Yasu's "pocket bell" (pager) from a payphone and told him I would leave Sado early... somehow.

As the long August days of worshiping the dead ended, I took my final afternoon run, but instead of running away from my life—pushing myself to the brink—I skipped up the hill for a short distance and then turned to cross a wide valley of rice paddies that overlooked the town. Midway I stopped and admired the flow of an irrigation stream. It was nothing special, but I wanted to take in a few simple views—sights of lovely simplicity that would remain with me as lasting memories of the "real Japan" that had so captured my heart.

As I stood there mesmerized by the rippling water, the cicada chorus that had ebbed and flowed throughout the summer afternoons began to grow in decibels from every direction. Without thinking I took off the delicate ankle bracelet I had bought to wear with the minis and threw it into the water. This was a spontaneous act, essentially without purpose or meaning. I did it to observe the gold glistening under the clear mountain water and because… well…just because I could.

In order to follow through with my plans to see both Yuki and Yasu, I would need two extra, unscheduled days in Tokyo. It was obvious that Satoko wasn't pleased at this turn of events.

As we were preparing to leave, Right's mother confronted me. My behavior of the summer had not gone unnoticed.

"School has changed you. You are holding your chin up too high," she told me in an unabashedly accusatory tone. "You should stop studying and pay more attention to your family."

Apparently she was of the opinion that my philosophy studies had gone to my head. I stepped down into my shoes before I replied.

"I want to graduate. I want to think for myself."

Satoko grimaced. "You know how Right is. You can't do just anything."

I felt a bit angry and somehow betrayed. Right had treated his own mother so poorly. How many times hadn't she confided in me regarding her son's deficient character? She knew my situation well. How could she expect me to just go on suffering? I was dealing with a problem she had essentially created.

"Is that fair? Can't I live a normal life?" I asked. "Can't I say and do what I think is best?"

Satoko was stern. "It is your job to be a good wife and mother. You made your choices, and you have to stick with them."

With this she rose and went down the hall. I heard her open the heavy door of the fireproof tower. With this I went out to load our bags in the car.

When I came back for the kids, Right's mother handed me a money envelope, the kind used for gifts.

"When you get to Tokyo, buy something more presentable to wear. You cannot go back to Right in the dresses you have been wearing around here."

I handed the envelope back. Knowing what I was about to do, I couldn't accept it. "I have enough cash. I have my credit card. Moreover, I like what I'm wearing."

Right's mother grabbed my forearm forcefully and thrust the envelope into my hand. "Change your image before you see Right," she instructed me in an imperious tone.

Further refusal was pointless. I deposited the money in my purse, picked up my backpack, and called for the children.

I felt bad for having been so tough with Satoko. It hadn't been my style to argue with her or to push back. I'm sure she had set out to be a good mother but for whatever reason had been unable to raise a son who appreciated her efforts. For this she had suffered and was about to endure more anguish with my departure. *All I could do was move forward quickly and not look back. In a few days I would have to do the same with Right. One way or another, I wouldn't be stuck.*

As the children slipped on their shoes, I took one last look at the little bit of the house I could see from the entryway. As the famous Sado song goes, Sado was easy living—a good place to live—but under the circumstances I couldn't stay.

Hours later I was in Tokyo, dragging the children from store to store. If Sado had been unusually hot that summer, Tokyo was unbearable. It was hard to breathe in the thick city air, but I had with me the equivalent of a thousand dollars to spend on "changing my image," and I was going to spend it. In the end I purchased a $400 dress and a $300 watch. These were frivolous expenditures, I knew, but I had taken on an attitude with the order to "look nice for Right" and decided to buy what I wanted, regardless of the price tag. In the end my shopping exhausted the kids—precisely my plan.

That night in the adjacent hotel room, I shed the baggage of fourteen years. It was as though Yasu and I had returned to the lodge loft at Kurohime camp and finished what we had started.

Yuki and I met the next day. Her face hadn't changed, but she was alarmingly thin. Nobu was between the ages of Gorgeous and Great, and the three of them downed their Happy Meals quickly before heading for the ball pit. We chose McDonalds for the very purpose of keeping the children occupied while the two of us caught up.

We had been teenagers the last time we had talked about "boys," but I needed to tell someone about what I had just done in order to gain perspective on what was about to occur. As the kids played I filled in Yuki on the details, telling her how wonderful it was to be with Yasu again, though regardless of what happened with him I was going to move forward with leaving Right.

That night after returning to the hotel I called Yasu, wanting him to know how I felt about our encounter of the night before. I told him I felt cleansed and whole, to the degree that I wouldn't let my husband touch me ever again.

But Yasu's tone had drastically changed.

"*Mattakumou!*" he cried out—the equivalent of "For crying out loud!" He was clearly not happy with me.

"What about your husband?" Yasu asked. "You have to sleep with him!"

"Never!" I answered firmly.

"You can't get away with that. You are his wife!" Yasu argued.

Yasu's reaction was nothing like what I had expected. Was he telling me to go home and do my duty? *Really?* I thought he would be happy in his conquest, elated that the man who had taken his girlfriend would in his turn be left in the lurch. Not so.

"I'm divorcing him. I can't stay with him another minute."

Yasu's frustration grew. "Stop saying that! You know I'm not going to marry you or anything like that. You *do* know this, don't you?"

Reality check. *Yes, I knew.* I had never personally met or heard of a man in Japan marrying a divorced woman with children. And, although I knew they existed, I had never actually met a divorcee in all my time there. I held out hope that Yasu was a different breed. He was, after all, the younger son of two. Maybe I was coming off as too intense too soon. I backed off.

"I know, Yasu. I know that. I just hope I can see you sometimes...once a year would be really nice."

"Stacy, listen! I cannot be involved in your decision to divorce. You understand that? What you are doing has nothing to do with me."

I told him I understood but that I had been planning to leave my husband even before I had left the United States, which wasn't exactly true. I had wanted to get out, and Yasu had given me the fortitude to actually do it. With my transgression functioning somehow as "permission," I could now face Right and make the break. Sure, it could have been anyone, but the fact that Yasu was my first love made it all so much easier.

Yasu asked what I was planning to do, and I told him I was going to graduate from college and get a job. This seemed to calm him down; I could hear him light a cigarette and take a drag.

In the course of our short reconnection, I'd learned that Yasu's good friends called him by another name, and I asked permission to use the moniker.

"Ya-chan?" The sound of his nickname was so endearing as it left my lips. "What is your very favorite song?"

He took another long drag. "Shima Uta," he answered without hesitation.

"Island Song?" I translated.

I hadn't heard of it, but I told him I would buy a copy the next morning on my way to catch the train.

After a long pause I called his nickname once more.

"Ya-chan…I have always loved you," I confessed. "I've thought about you every day since Kurohime. I couldn't forget your address even when I tried."

"Me too," he replied softly, "but we are only friends."

The next day before boarding the express for the airport, I bought a cassette tape of "Island Song." As my children sat next to me, oblivious to the fact that their world was about to change forever, I pulled out the cassette and listened.

The island song rides the wind,
And crosses the ocean with the birds.
The island song rides the wind,
I pray my love reaches you.

The entire song was about long-distance love. And, of course, I wondered… obviously I wondered, was this just a catchy tune, or did it mean something more to my love?

Right was smiling when he approached us at Detroit Metro. I experienced a twinge of sympathy for the man but still felt strong enough to follow through. Ten minutes after we had walked into the house and settled the kids in the TV room, I confronted Right in the kitchen.

"I have something to tell you," I said, keeping my voice low.

"Yeah? What's that?"

"I'm leaving you. It's over."

Right's jaw dropped, his face registering utter shock.

"What are you talking about? What are you saying?" He repeated my words in complete disbelief, as though they weren't registering.

"I have decided I want a divorce. I want you out of this house as soon as possible," I informed him matter-of-factly. My sweet tone, my little girl voice was completely gone. I could hardly recognize myself as toxins spewed from my mouth.

I took a step backward, fully expecting the kitchen to erupt into a war zone. Counters were about to be cleared—anything within reach smashed. I was mentally prepared for the most horrendous blow up of our marriage, but nothing moved.

"What happened, huh? What happened in Japan? *Tell me!*" Right demanded.

"I did something…and I did it because of *you!*" I kept my voice low so the children wouldn't hear, but I pronounced every word with conviction and strength.

"What? Tell me what you are talking about!" Right was starting to lose patience.

I paused and drew a deep breath, summoning fortitude. Then I told him that I'd slept with the "bad boy."

Right, incredulous, challenged my claim.

"Oh, trust me, it's true." My voice dripped sarcasm. "All these years you told me I was stupid! All your evil stares! Making me tiptoe around you! You and your collection! I hate you and everything you've done to me!"

Right was still in denial. "Where? How?"

"At the Tourist Hotel. I got an extra room. Go ahead and call the hotel if you don't believe me. Ask how many rooms I had Friday night. I had two!"

I let my anger flow unimpeded. Years of contempt poured from my mouth like an icy shower. If the children hadn't been in the house, I would have been the one screaming and breaking things. I had turned the tables.

Right, shell-shocked, denied that he had ever cheated on me—a claim I found ludicrous. He just couldn't find anyone young enough now that he was approaching his late thirties.

"You would have done it with *my sister* if she had responded to you! Don't lie. You just didn't have the opportunity! And I never gave you any reason to do it! I was good to you, and I never refused you!"

Right said nothing, but I wasn't finished. I stabbed my finger in the air in his direction, pantomiming knifelike, airborne jabs.

"*You* have created this situation. You raped me over and over again with your words and actions! You said horrible things to me!"

"You are breaking up our family!" he cried, oblivious to my accusations.

He must have realized he was dealing with a completely different person, that his usual tactics of intimidation, belittling, and breaking things weren't going to work. He was trying to guilt-trip me.

"*No! You* broke our family! Get that straight! You never loved me for me! You wanted to make me into someone younger, someone completely obedient! It's worse now that I'm old!"

There was a pause. Right was clearly at a loss, completely unprepared for this level of defiance.

"So, what are you planning to do?" he asked finally.

"I want you *out of here*. I'm going to see a lawyer. I don't want you near me. Stay very far from me. I will call the police if you step near me or break anything in this house."

After I had given Right his walking orders, he retreated to the second floor. I waited for the door to slam and the sounds of destruction to begin, but all I could hear was the TV in the other room—the opening song of one of the children's favorite Japanese children's shows: "There is a happy, happy island where there are happy, happy friends."

The next day Right didn't go to work. I didn't see him until he came down after dinner to get a glass of water, at which time he kept his head down and didn't look at me.

"There's some dinner left in the refrigerator if you want it," I informed him.

"I don't want anything," Right replied in a monotone as he shuffled across the kitchen. He was in his pajamas. "I don't want to live."

I felt no sympathy for him. How many times hadn't I told him I was so sad I wanted to die, and he had *laughed*? Now our roles had been completely reversed.

"Well, that's your problem now, isn't it?" I called after him.

These words had practically been coined by Right. How many times hadn't he told me that my sadness and depression were my problems?

Right stopped at the bottom of the stairs and looked at me. "I can't believe you would do this to our family and our kids."

He still didn't get it. I reminded him that everything that was happening was his fault. Up until this day any hint of insubordination on my part would have brought the house down. It felt eerie. *When would he snap?*

Then, just as I was contemplating what to say next, Right himself said something I hadn't heard since the summer after our marriage when I had briefly moved out.

"I'm sorry," he conceded, his voice a cross between a whine and real contrition. "I've made some mistakes."

To this I responded coldly that it was too little, too late. I told him that if I had ever thought he could change I wouldn't have taken the desperate actions I had.

With this Right left the room, but later on that evening he resurfaced.

"If there's nothing I can do, then I have decided to go back to Sado."

This was great news. I could really get him out of my life. I was feeling proud of myself—until he let the bomb drop.

"I'm going to kill myself on Sado."

This was the first time Right had ever said anything about suicide. I should have been sympathetic, consoling at this point, but I couldn't let my guard down.

"Huh?" I responded, imitating his typical guttural huff. "Go ahead then."

The next day, as I thought through Right's request, I came to the conclusion that I shouldn't be involved in his plan. For the children's sake I proceeded to convince Right that they needed him.

Right eventually returned to his office and I to school. From the outside no one probably suspected a thing, but the children were beginning to ask questions. Their father was staying out of sight, and the few times he appeared before them he was in tears. I had to tell them that he would be moving out.

Sitting on Gorgeous's bed, I talked to both children in straightforward terms about their father, or "To-chan," as they called him.

"Mama cannot live with To-chan anymore," I began.

Immediately there was protest from Gorgeous. "No mama! *No!*" Instantly she began to cry.

Great was calm. "Why, Mama?" he asked simply. "Because To-chan always gets mad at you?"

I had always tried to keep peace by being "good," but they had seen him snap often enough.

"Yes. I make mistakes," I went on, "and your To-chan gets mad. Mama is tired of trying to make To-chan happy. Do you understand?"

Great said he did. "Like when To-chan threw his beer mug and it broke on the fireplace and then he smashed the dishes *like this?*"

"I'm sorry you remember that, baby."

"I remember lots of broken dishes, Mama. There was glass and food everywhere. To-chan was real mad."

"Yes. Since Mama is too tired and can't do things like To-chan wants, we'll have to look for an apartment for him."

Both children protested.

"Don't worry. We'll look together and find a very nice apartment nearby. You can see To-chan any time you like."

Great asked a hundred more questions, and with each answer he seemed to further adjust. His older sister—Ne-chan, as he called her—had nothing more to say. She was rolled up in a ball, crying.

Over the next few days, Right tried to change my mind several times. He attempted to make impractical deals that had us remaining in the same house but maintaining separate lives. It was all nonsense. I really couldn't stand the sight of him.

Soon after Right's move Sado called. They were looking for Right. I informed Satoko that he had his own apartment and provided the number.

Satoko expressed shock but sounded as though she had seen it coming. She was quick enough, though, to blame it on me and my "too much nonsense philosophy."

As school started life got easier for the three of us. At the end of our day, we could come home and relax to some degree. I was less tense and relaxed some of the rules for the children. I didn't have to worry constantly about petty details. They still played with their Mazda friends, and I continued to drink tea with the wives. I had been concerned that they would shun us, but this didn't happen. A couple of them were actually quite supportive of my situation, without requesting much explanation.

Despite his warnings before I had left Tokyo, indicating that he wanted nothing to do with my divorce, Yasu called the house frequently to check on my welfare. A few weeks into the fall semester I received letter 121...or something like that.

Dear Stacy,

How are you? I hope you are always in good health and happy! I'm fine, but very busy. I'm very sorry I cannot write letters often, but I have not forgotten about you…every day…every night.

How is Michigan's climate? Japan is gradually getting cooler and fall-like. What you said on the phone recently…I couldn't sleep thinking of your words. Really, it's true. I'm writing this letter at my company because I don't have a desk at my house to write letters. I'm sorry I can't write many letters to you.

Now it is 10:30 a.m. in Japan, so it is about 9:30 p.m. in Michigan. Are you studying hard? Perhaps you are sleeping? How were your tests this week? Someone who tries hard like you, Stacy, is sure to have done well. These days I don't really study at all. Occasionally I have to study something related to my work. Ha-ha. Construction regulations or something like that…but for someone with a head as bad as mine…it is a losing cause.

Tomorrow I'm going fishing with a couple of guys from work. It will be the first time I've been fishing in quite a while. I'm looking forward to it.

By the way, can you come to Japan soon? When can you come? When you come in my arms again, I'm never going to separate from you, okay?
October 20, 1994
So Long.
Yasu

CHAPTER 11

Binging on Culture

I had been an exchange student in Tokyo, a bride on Sado, a caregiver to a dying Japanese grandmother, and an "education mama," raising my children firmly in the culture. Now I was going to be something else—a jet-setting karaoke queen.

I LEFT THE CHILDREN WITH Right for a long weekend, telling him I was under a lot of stress with school and that I needed to get out of town for a while. I told him I was going to Northern Michigan—not sure exactly where I would be stopping or staying. I was just going. I don't think Right would ever have guessed that I was catching a plane to Japan. After all, I had just been there with the children. And...who goes so far for three nights? *It was Ya-chan's seductive words that lured me. He had my drug, and I simply couldn't resist.*

As planned, right on time, there he was, standing near the landmark clock at Kawasaki Station. Yasu was wearing a dark blue business suit, and his hair was slicked back, looking all professional. I had to do a double take, but as soon as our eyes met I knew it was him. I waved and began walking in his direction. As I did, Yasu turned away from me and took off.

Following my lover, I pushed forward through the crisscrossing paths of commuters, but I couldn't catch him. I kept Yasu in my sights, but he was moving fast. When I reached the outside Yasu stood waiting a few feet ahead. Motioning toward a dark green sedan, he hopped in. Only when I was inside the car did Yasu act as though he knew me.

"Did you have any trouble getting the train from the airport?" he asked, handing me a stick of gum.

"No, not at all," I answered. "I'm getting used to them."

"You can speak Japanese, so it's no problem for you. Since the days I wrote you all of those letters I've forgotten English. If I became lost in America I would be in trouble."

Ya-chan turned on the radio. His choice was an oldies pop station.

"Do you know this song?" he asked.

Right wasn't into Japanese pop music at all, so I hadn't kept up on the latest. I replied that I only knew *doyo*—children's songs, and a lot of them. With this Yasu named a title and challenged me to sing it. My rendition impressed him. I decided to turn the tables.

"Do you know the "Demon Pants" song?"

Ya-chan admitted that he did not.

I sang Great's favorite song—one we'd learned at Cabbage Club—a little routine complete with hand motions that demonstrated how wonderfully strong demon pants are and how everyone should wear a pair. It always made Great double over in laughter, no matter how many times we sang it.

Suddenly I felt a wave of sadness washing over me. At that moment, for a split second, I felt regret, as though I shouldn't have been sitting in that car.

"Stacy? *Daijoubu?*" ("Are you okay?")

I was startled. "What? Yes. I'm fine," I responded, covering my mouth to stifle a yawn. "Tired. Too much study."

Ya-chan searched for a new channel and hit upon rock.

"You like?" he asked.

We were making idle chitchat and getting along when Ya-chan suddenly pulled over.

Without a word he jumped from the car and disappeared into a bank. A few minutes later I saw him dash out and then run across the street to a convenience store. He returned with two sandwiches and two cans of hot coffee. The one with cream was for me.

Coffee in hand, Ya-chan merged onto Chuo Freeway, passing several cars as he entered. I asked about his driving record.

He laughed. "Oh, several accidents...but all of them were minor scrapes. I scratched my car on the concrete walls around our house when I was drunk. Minor stuff."

"I thought Japan was strict about driving drunk," I put in, puzzled.

"They are...but I never get caught," he said with a boyish grin. "I'm careful; don't worry."

After an hour on the highway, Ya-chan pulled off. I asked where he was planning to take me.

"Sightseeing, of course!" he replied, raising his caterpillar-like brows.

Now Ya-chan sounded like my father. When I was a kid my dad would often announce that we were going for a drive but would never say exactly where. It annoyed me then, but in this case I appreciated Yasu's take charge ways. I trusted he was trying to please me.

We drove through a valley and then began ascending a steep hill. Halfway up Ya-chan pulled over, parked at a self-serve rest stop, and motioned for me to get out.

Peering out over a rail, he sighed, "Aww...It's too hazy to see Mt. Fuji. It should be over there." He pointed off into the distance.

"Too cloudy," I agreed.

Ya-chan sauntered off toward a little shack of vending machines and returned with two more cans of coffee. Nudging me with his shoulder, he handed me one. This was a gesture to break the ice; up to that point he had been all business.

We continued our ascent until we reached a large plateau where dozens of cars were parked. Ya-chan got out of the car, and I followed.

The landscape was filled with lava craters and bellowing steam, and the air smelled putrid. All around people were peeling and eating boiled eggs. Ya-chan explained that the eggs were cooked by the steam and considered good for one's health, so each of us ate two for stamina.

The sightseeing portion of our evening complete, we forged on, enjoying a nice dinner and drinks before searching for just the right place to stay. For years I had wondered why certain hotels in Japan had large, fortress-like walls and gates. I was about to learn.

After requesting admission through an intercom, we pulled in and selected a carport that was connected to a white plaster hut. *Was there no front desk, no check in?* I wondered.

Once inside I felt as though I'd been teleported to Hugh Hefner's *Playboy* mansion. As I looked around, I heard a voice call out. Looking around, I saw no one, though finally I realized that the voice had come from a mail slot in the door. Then I noticed a hand, palm upright, protruding from the same.

Ya-chan scurried to pull several bills from his wallet and placed them in the open hand. Apparently satisfied, without so much as an *arigato* ("thank you"), the hand retreated, the flap closing behind it. *This was a hotel built specifically for liaisons.*

When I had daydreamed about my weekend trip, I had pictured a romantic seaside B and B or a mountain hot springs resort...not some trampy, windowless hotel—but then again this was Japan, and apparently "love hotels" were the places people like us were destined to go for our business. As the evening wound down and our glasses of whiskey turned to water, Ya-chan naturally drifted off. Beside him I lay wide awake, staring at the pitch black ceiling and wondering how I would escape should a fire ignite from the stray ashes.

The next morning we opened the door of our dark, windowless bungalow to a beautiful but foggy November morning. For this day Ya-chan had planned a drive up Mt. Fuji, but the visibility wouldn't permit it.

We drove around killing time and waiting for the fog to lift, but when it didn't we began looking for something else to do. As we were driving along, Ya-chan abruptly made a U-turn and drove a short distance before pointing up toward a billboard. Apparently there was an amusement park nearby.

"Let's go!" he enthused. "It's been a long time since I've gone to a *yuuenchi!*"

I protested that rides made me sick, but Ya-chan assured me these would be mellow.

At the park we rode tiny coasters, raced go-carts, and whipped around in little whirl-a-gig rides of all kinds. And then, just when I thought we'd done everything, Ya-chan suggested we enter a log maze.

The goal of the gigantic maze was to hit certain checkpoints where you would stamp a timecard with letters that spelled "H-O-W." After obtaining all of the stamps you had to exit before your opponent in order to win.

Examining the map posted at the entrance, I could tell that the maze was massive. Once inside there would be no way for us to get our bearings except by looking over the large log walls from atop one of the two bridges at the far corners. Feeling confident, I turned to Ya-chan and threw out a challenge.

"I have a great sense of direction, you know. I never get lost, even in places I've never been. I'm definitely going to be the winner!"

With this bold claim I punched my timecard and took off around the first corner. At every turn I expected to see Ya-chan, but we didn't cross paths until several minutes later. Sauntering toward me, he smugly asked how many stamps I'd collected.

"None!" I replied, as though he were asking a stupid question.

"Ha!" he barked out smugly, holding up his card.

My eyes widened in a comic look of shock. He had the dang "H." I turned on my heels and dashed back around the corner I had just rounded. Maybe I had missed a critical turn.

It was November, and the amusement park was nearly empty. Ya-chan and I were alone in the maze. In fact, if not for one other couple and a group of teenage boys who occasionally walked by us between rides, we would have been completely alone. The low attendance was undoubtedly due to the weather. It was nearly as cold and damp in Hakone as on any fall day in Michigan.

I scampered between walls looking for the stamp stations, but my altered state clouded my ability to navigate. I was high again—binging on culture and sleeping with my preferred dealer. In order to win I was betting on sheer speed and luck.

At last I found one of the lookout bridges. As I peered over the maze, I yelled to Ya-chan on the other side. "Still one stamp?"

"Two!" He replied, grinning.

One hundred turns later I finally got my first stamp...the "O." I had no idea where the "H" station might be. After fifteen or twenty more minutes of scurrying, I found another overpass bridge. Ya-chan was nowhere to be found.

"Obaa here yo!" ("Hey, over here!") Ya-chan called.

My savvy city rat had sniffed his way to the cheese and was grinning in all his glory near the exit sign. I squatted down, holding the rail of the bridge and laughing at my stupidity. I had lost to a streetwise scavenger.

After another thirty minutes of wandering around alone in the maze, hopelessly lost and still missing my "H," I had to cry uncle. From a lookout point I yelled across to Ya-chan that I was stuck.

The maze had looked so simple when I had seen it on the entrance map, but it turned out to be very complex. How could Ya-chan, a man who never seemed to care about intellectual pursuit, have navigated his way through the course as though he were on a Sunday stroll? I was dumbfounded by the level of his instinct.

Before leaving the park, Ya-chan stopped in front of a coin-stamping machine and deposited several hundred yen into a slot. When commanded by the machine he chose a gold-colored coin from the selection of three designs and began to type his message: "Stacy and Yasu." After the coin pressed and released, Ya-chan turned and placed it in my right palm. "A souvenir for you, my Stacy."

That night, the second of my trip, Ya-chan suggested we turn in early at a Western style hotel and rest. Again I did not sleep.

The next day, before dropping me off to catch my train to the airport, Ya-chan admonished me for being "too serious." After counseling me not to "overthink" our relationship, he was quick to tack on a "Come back to me soon" invitation.

On the basis of the time change, I arrived in Michigan before I had left Japan, without having slept for the entire trip. My incoherence, along with the unusual brevity of my stay, made me an easy target for the customs agent.

"Why were you in Japan again?" he asked, flipping through my passport.

"I told you. I went to visit a friend."

"It looks like you go to Japan often? You went twice in the last few months, and you're just going for fun?"

I told the agent I had a lot of friends there, but, confused by the fact that I was a student without a job, he threatened to have my body cavities searched. Too exhausted to make a fuss, I told him I didn't really care.

Finally, after retrieving my shoes from the other side of the x-ray machine, I was allowed to pass. I drove straight to pick up my babies, studied Kant's position on metaphysics till midnight, and went to school the next day.

Right lived in an apartment in the next town, just a few miles away from the house and his office. Our divorce was in the works, and for the most part he wasn't fighting it. In a rush to be done with everything, I drew simple lines in the sand and tried to be agreeable. There was little to no argument on the division of property. Right wanted the house, and I didn't. Nor did we fight over the children. I had physical custody, and Right had them nearly every weekend.

Weekends were lonely for me. I studied all day, but by the time night fell and I could no longer think logically enough to continue, a deep sadness would come over me. I often drank alone in our big quiet house, watching MTV until I fell asleep. This was my routine until I found Izakaya Sanpei.

Pub Sanpei was one of the three original Japanese restaurants in the western suburbs that had come to support the burgeoning Japanese transplant population, and according to one of my Mazda housewife friends it had a good karaoke selection. I had never thought I could sing, but Yasu had given me a cassette from his car, '80s Japanese pop mix that seemed vocally doable.

Over and over I practiced songs by Nakamori, Akina (formal Japanese places the last name first). Although her voice and look had been candy when she had debuted in the early eighties, just after the iconic "Mastuda, Seiko" (*the original "cutey idol" Japanese girls of my generation sought to emulate*), Akina quickly ditched her soft, feathered hair and frilly pink dresses for an edgier look, her voice becoming grittier at the same time. "Kita Wing," a song about long-distance love, was my debut piece.

After getting over my initial stage fright, I began practicing more, and every week brought a new song. In short order I became a *jyorenkyaku*, a regular guest who received special treats from the sushi chefs. Many times after singing I'd be invited over to tables and enjoy free drinks. One night, after too many cocktails, I awoke to a strange combination of smells. Fish, alcohol, and body odor indicated that I was not alone.

I kept this indiscretion to myself. At this point I was leading multiple Japanese lives: a doting Japanese mother on the weekdays, a karaoke queen on the weekends, and a jet-setting lover whenever possible. In between I was a full-time college student. I was burning cedar incense at both ends on the altar of culture.

The little chef was my first real "oops" but was not to be my last. Soon enough I had a super fan: a younger Japanese engineer in Detroit on a temporary work visa.

The young man, whose name was "Ito, Kouji," wore Air Nikes and skinny jeans and sported a single diamond stud in his left ear. I estimated that he was at least five years my junior. Always looking for someone of my persuasion (Japanese) to talk to, I hit it off with Kouji. As I always did at Sanpei, however, I kept my true identity a secret. The Japanese community in Detroit was big, but not that big. I didn't want news of my crazy Saturday nights getting back to anyone from Mazda or to Right.

Despite my elusive behavior, Kouji expressed an interest in visiting "my place" and learning more about me. There were many problems with his request. He had no idea I was technically still married (though not for long) and that I had children. He was also unaware of my jet-setting tendencies—not to mention that it was spring break and I was about to leave for Tokyo again.

Yuki had agreed to meet me for coffee on the night of my arrival, and the two of us decided on decadent coffee jelly with whipped cream and chocolate syrup. As we played with the last few coffee cubes at the bottoms of our parfait glasses, I told my sister that although I was glad for the chance to see her I wished I'd never made the trip.

"I came all this way to see Ya-chan, and now I feel like I shouldn't. He's like whiskey and ice," I shared. "Strong and smooth going down, but the aftereffects are hard on my mind."

Yuki must have thought I was nuts, having just traveled halfway around the world.

Stabbing at my last jelly cube, I sighed heavily. "Yuki, I'm scared."

My sister looked at me. "Maybe he loves you, but he can't do anything about it. He can't really love you back because of the past and because of his parents."

This made total sense, but it wasn't at all gratifying. As I began walking back to the hotel, I felt intense regret. I wanted to go home, but I was stuck. I'd never felt that way in Japan before...homesick. Feeling anxious and alone, I turned on my heels and headed for the train station.

I was expecting a barrage of flashing lights and herds of young people when I reached Tokyo's party district of Roppongi, but the streets were quiet. After walking in circles for about thirty minutes, I felt cold and wished I were back in my hotel room.

As I headed back to the station, though, I sensed that someone was following me. When I picked up my pace, the footsteps behind me also quickened. Finally, unable to bear the suspense, I stopped and turned around. My eyes met those of a tall, thin stranger.

"Why are you alone in a place like this?" he asked.

I told him I wanted to dance and was looking for a club.

"It's dangerous to walk around here alone, and moreover, it's cold," he pointed out. "Why don't you step inside my *sunakku*? I just closed it, but for you, I'll open it up again."

A *sunakku* was a tiny, intimate bar. I'd never been inside one and was culturally curious.

Kondo (as he introduced himself) led me around several corners to what appeared to be an office building. From there we ascended a couple of flights of stairs and proceeded through two sets of locked doors to another, unassuming entrance.

"I didn't have a customer today, so I closed early," he explained.

"Not even one?" I asked.

"No," he responded. "So welcome!"

Kondo got behind the counter and offered me a drink, and as I was sipping he began preparing a light dish. Between the chopping and frying he asked me why I was in Japan and how it was I spoke Japanese so well.

Having nothing to hide, I felt free to admit the details of what was going on. I told him about my twelve-year marriage, my beautiful children, my pending divorce, and the reason for my trip. Unabashedly I shared the nature of my relationship with Yasu, and even my fears.

Kondo's opinion was that if Ya-chan were a real man in love, nothing should keep him from being with me. A real man would accept my situation and stand up for me in front of his parents. I couldn't agree more, but I also knew that Japan isn't America. There wasn't a large population of Japanese men willing to take on divorced women—let alone women with children who were *gaijin* to boot.

After eating a simple stir-fry, we turned on the disco ball and began to karaoke, each singing a few solos and wrapping up the evening with a duet. As Kondo walked me back to the station, he asked about my plans for the next day, whether I intended to follow through with seeing the man of whom I had spoken. When I told him I wasn't sure, he handed me his business card.

"Well, if you decide not to meet him," Kondo said, "give me a call. Staying at a hotel in Tokyo can be expensive, and I have room for you if you want to stay at my place."

The next day I went to Kawasaki station at the agreed upon time and found Yasu waiting in the same spot near the big clock. As soon as I spotted my old flame and our eyes met, Yasu turned away and took off, just as he'd done the last time we had met up. This time I was determined to catch up before he got outside.

Sprinting through the crowd, I kept my eye on the elusive Ya-chan until I was directly behind him. Grabbing his forearm, I placed a note in his hand and then took off in the opposite direction. This time I wouldn't be going to some stinking, smutty love hotel.

On way back into Tokyo from Kawasaki, I felt myself to be out of my mind. I had dreamed of spending time with my old friend but had completely thrown away our weekend in a rash decision. Now I was stuck, not to mention dog tired—with neither a hotel reservation nor an agenda. I piddled away the remainder of the day shopping for new karaoke CDs and other cultural paraphernalia, but it felt meaningless. It was in this state that I decided to take up Kondo on his offer.

Kondo's place didn't offer the accommodations I'd been expecting. As he led me from the train station to his abode I was surprised to see that he didn't use a key to enter.

"You don't lock your door?" I asked, incredulous.

"No." He brushed off my concern with a dismissive gesture. "I lost my key, and the landlord would charge me for another. I don't have anything worth taking anyway. Don't be shocked. My apartment is small."

This was indeed the case. It was a six-mat—a nine-foot-by-nine-foot room with a small kitchen attached. There was a toilet, but no shower or bath. I asked how he managed to live without anywhere to bathe, and he informed me that he used a nearby public facility and would take me there.

As Kondo rummaged around for bathing supplies, I took a seat on the only bare spot of tatami I could find. Unsure I was really sitting where I seemed to be—in a complete stranger's six-mat somewhere on the outskirts of Tokyo—I could barely feel my body. I wanted to be somewhere else, anywhere else, but I lacked the energy to think, let alone move.

Yet apparently I did move—for the sake of a bath; half an hour later there I was, ass naked in front of a couple of dozen neighborhood women and girls, all of them side-eyeing me as though I were a freak. Under ordinary circumstances this might have bothered me; as it was I didn't care. At that moment all I wanted was to be clean...and away from men. The reprieve, though, was short.

An hour later I found myself back at Kondo's six-mat, where he offered me a shot of whiskey to ward off the cold. Not only did he not have a key, he seemed not to own a space heater of any kind. I accepted the whiskey, figuring that I needed it from multiple perspectives—least of which was the fact that I was cold. This was one night I would have to forget.

As I sipped Kondo talked about his various money-making ventures, as well as his acceptance of Christ through some cultish-sounding sect I'd never heard of. During our conversation the phone rang twice. One of the calls was regarding a debt he owed, the other about some job he had scheduled for the next day.

At last it was time to turn out the lights. Kondo made a small space, pulled out his bedding, and arranged the futon. The blankets were noticeably filthy, and it was clear that there was room for only one. I looked at the time—realizing with a sinking feeling that the trains were about to stop for the night.

"Kondo, please listen to me. I've told you about the problems in my life. You can't imagine how tired my mind is at this moment. You aren't going to bother me tonight, are you?" I was practically pleading.

Kondo tilted his head upward and laughed so hard I thought he was going to howl. His buckteeth were almost parallel with the floor, and I could see his gums.

"You are an attractive woman and an interesting person. Do you really expect me not to make a move on you?" he asked, as though intending to convince me of how ludicrous that sounded.

"I thought you were a gentleman," I replied, my senses on red alert despite my aching weariness.

"Stacy, what did you expect? It's natural. It would make me feel much better, and…*gosh!* I haven't had sex in three years. Think of it as a favor to a friend."

I was cornered.

"Please let me sleep, Kondo. You said you're a Christian. Anything against my will is rape and a sin. Do you agree?" I was grasping at straws, thinking that perhaps I could use Kondo's professed beliefs to control him.

There was no response. Kondo turned out the lights.

The next day I made it back to the city and booked a room at the Tourist Hotel for two nights. I was going to rest and study. As wasteful as it was to travel so far and do nothing but what I could have done at home, I had to stop moving. I settled in for the afternoon and evening with a bottle of wine and some boxed food. As darkness fell the room phone rang.

"*What is wrong with you!*" The voice on the other end bellowed. "Don't you know I've been looking for you!"

I didn't have an answer.

"Who travels so far to see someone and then runs off? Don't you think you're becoming a little crazy?"

Ya-chan was understandably annoyed.

"Stacy, you know we cannot go back in time. We can pretend, but it will never be like it was when we were sixteen."

I protested, arguing that I couldn't take it if he ended up marrying someone else after everything we'd experienced together, but Ya-chan advised me that such matters were out of his hands, that family and societal expectations were at play. He followed this up with a request to see me at my usual hotel and closed the conversation with a casual "love you."

The next day I was back in Michigan putting on a good face in front of my children. After picking them up from their father's apartment, making a good dinner, and putting them to bed, I collapsed on the living room floor. I wasn't sick per se, but I had binged on culture for a week; beginning with the previous Saturday night at pub Sanpei, I had been continuously used and was coming down in a bad way.

Lying in the shallow pool of my regretful existence, I fell asleep. Sometime later I was jarred awake by the sound of the ringing phone.

"Oh, you have returned!" It was Kouji, the karaoke fan.

I fudged. "Just now, actually."

"How was your trip?" he asked.

Scenes of Kondo and Ya-chan flashed before me. "Boring, actually...I wish I hadn't gone."

The Sanpei fan asked where I lived; he wanted to stop by. In my stupor I told him I was too tired but that perhaps the next evening would work.

I was running on fumes. Getting through the day was hard enough without the added pressure of anticipating a guest that evening, but I reckoned it was time to tell my fan the truth about my situation. He needed to know that I was technically the wife of a Mazda engineer (for another month anyway) and the mother of two. I had gone to Sanpei because I was lonely and wanted to be with others whom I considered to be of like kind.

Kouji appeared at my door just after Gorgeous and Great had fallen asleep. Even as I let him in, I was sure he would notice signs of my real life: the small shoes staged in the *genkan*, the photo collages that lined the hall to the *chanoma*, children's books on the shelves. If Kouji did notice these things he didn't let on. After a few minutes of beating around the bush, I told him the truth about my life. Not surprisingly, he was perturbed.

"Who are you? Are you hunting Japanese guys?"

I assured him that this wasn't the case—that I had been going to Sanpei because it felt natural to me. I wouldn't consider hanging out in an American bar because I wouldn't know what to expect or how to relate to people.

The next day I settled back into my student/mother life. I swore to myself that I was going to stay away from trouble, avoid Sanpei, and definitely *not* venture again to Japan, at least not for a long time. I knew it would be one day at a time, but I was resolved. Resolved, that is, for the time it took for the doorbell to ring. I opened the door to a surprising visitor—the young fan.

It seemed that Kouji had done some soul searching and had come to the conclusion that he wanted to get to know me—and my children—a little better. He claimed that he felt weak for not having been more understanding. He asked some basic details about my children, and I was happy for the chance to talk about them.

Following this incident the young man and I became close—to the degree that he all but replaced Yasu as my source of affection and connection with Japan. Ya-chan still called, but gradually I created "mental distance" so I could be free to foster a relationship with Kouji. From my end I didn't call, and it took only a week or two before Yasu realized exactly what was going on. Once again he found himself on the short end of my increasingly fickle nature.

While Right and Yasu were on the taller side, Kouji was slight—five feet sixish, normal height for a Japanese man. Back home he enjoyed fishing and driving his Toyota pickup. Definitely more modern than either Right or Yasu, Kouji declared that he was free to marry anyone and live anywhere he wanted. In fact, he had considered living in the United States and had asked his supervisors about staying in Michigan longer, if not permanently. His youthful way of thinking was attractive to me, and gradually I came to depend on his stopping by and secretly spending the night. This situation lasted for a couple of months, during which my divorce became final.

I provided Kouji with everything he needed outside of work—everything from meals to laundry services, from interpretation and translation, to intimate companionship. But all was not well with this relationship. Kouji had a little secret in the form of a girlfriend back home—a much younger girl he was considering for marriage. Following his eventual confession of this fact, he disappeared from my life.

It had become my habit to drink wine after a long night of studying just to come down from all the brainwork. With Kouji gone my intake increased, and I took to adding sleeping pills into the mix. One night after I had taken more than a couple of pills, my old friend called. During my time with Kouji he had been quick to notice that there was some diversion in my life and had backed off.

Instead of being grateful that Yasu was calling at a time when I could really use the comfort of a friendly voice, I immediately accused him of doing so for his own pleasure. This, not surprisingly, didn't go over well.

"*You* are the one who left *me!* Twice now, isn't it?" Sounding exasperated, Ya-chan was clearly fed up with my antics. "And you are accusing *me* of playing?"

Yasu was spot on. I couldn't understand why he had even bothered to call. Frankly, I was lucky he was still in the picture at all. Given the circumstances I had to ask why it was he even cared. Instead of answering Yasu asked me to answer the same question first.

"It was the moon rabbits," I told him softly. "I couldn't forget those days."

He agreed that it was the same for him.

My heart was pounding hard. I was sweating and couldn't speak. After hearing Ya-chan utter "love you" under his breath, without saying good-bye, I hung up the phone.

A while later it rang again, and I fumbled to pick up the receiver.

"Are you really okay?" Ya-chan asked, his voice expressing real concern. "Stacy, I cannot go to Detroit at this moment—so please take care of yourself!"

The receiver fell from my hand. I experienced an odd sensation of hearing Ya-chan calling my name from a distance. At some point I picked up the receiver and lay it on the pillow against my head.

Ya-chan pleaded for me to listen and call him the next day when I awoke. I in turn asked why it was he cared. Once again he directed me to stop asking such questions, adding that we were "spiritual friends," forever linked. If I were to perish at some point before he did, he insisted that he would instinctually know.

"*Spiritual* friends?" I repeated. I liked the sound of that and wanted to hear him say it again—I needed clear affirmation, which my friend promptly supplied.

"You're the best," I whispered.

The next morning I woke to my alarm, got up robotically, and went to school. A few days later Kouji returned. As long as he was in Michigan he wanted to play things out.

CHAPTER 12

Living in the Six-Mat

And you may ask yourself, "Well…how did I get here?"
And you may ask yourself, "How do I work this?"
And you may ask yourself, "Where is that large automobile?"
And you may tell yourself, "This is not my beautiful house."

TALKING HEADS, "ONCE IN A LIFETIME," 1981

THE FIRST WEEKEND IN MAY 1995, I achieved one important goal and graduated with high distinction. This was everything I'd worked for during the previous two years, but it was about to mean very little. Stupidly, I had let time pass without doing what I needed to do for my children and our life moving forward, and everything was coming to a head.

Per the divorce decree the house was Right's, and I had until the end of the children's school year, just weeks, before we would have to move. While I should have been pursuing work and a place to live, I had done nothing but study, play, and drink. I was in deep trouble—and that's when things only got worse.

Even though I had been careful to hide Kouji's overnight visits from the children and Right, somehow our misdeeds were discovered, and Right quite naturally exploded. Given the fact that he was about to take the house from me anyway, I packed my things and moved out, instructed Right to take care of the kids for a while until I could find a suitable place to take them.

I stayed with Kouji for a couple of weeks until his visa expired, and from there I took up residence in an RV parked in my parents' driveway. It was my intention to figure things out—to find a job and secure a place for the kids—but that didn't happen. I had no clue what do with my degree in philosophy and no career aspirations. Quite justifiably, Right accused me of abandoning our children.

I went to Detroit every week to see the kids, but within a matter of a month they weren't the same children I had raised. Their once animated spirits were like shadows behind their robotic movements. Great indicated that he was being spanked regularly with a towel bar, and Gorgeous had been told she was stupid and drilled endlessly. My heart ached for them, but I felt sure there was nothing I could do. For the remainder of that summer I drank and ran; I had no sense of direction whatsoever.

As summer turned to fall, I eventually took a bilingual concierge job at an international hotel on the outskirts of Detroit. To cover the long drive to work I took a second job at a Japanese restaurant across the street from the hotel. Between jobs I drank and slept in my car. My existence was hanging by a thread.

One November day, struggling in all aspects of my life, I abruptly quit both jobs and boarded the next flight for Japan, telling the children I was visiting Yuki for a while.

Poor Yuki. I informed her from a Narita Airport payphone that I needed a place to stay. She responded gamely that she ordinarily got out of work at around 8:00 p.m. and that if I could catch a bus and make it to her office park she would pick me up.

I expected Yuki's son, Nobu, to be awake when we arrived, but he fallen asleep by the TV. Yuki informed me that he was watched in a kind of latchkey program after school but that since she seldom left work in time to retrieve him he usually went home alone, ate, and watched TV until he was tired. Being a single mother in Japan was a tough road, but she was somehow managing without assistance. Using a pager at first and then newer cellular technology, she had been somehow able to keep track of her boy.

Over late night coffee, I told Yuki all that had transpired since I had seen her last. I was terribly lost without my children and really struggling. Yuki didn't know how to respond but offered one of her two bedrooms for me to use; her son spent every night in her bed anyway. This, she shared, constituted the little bit of comfort she could provide Nobu during the weekdays.

Kouji had left Michigan without giving me any answers. He supposedly loved me and wanted to find a way to work and live in the United States, but he also said he was unsure of what he really wanted, and in the weeks and months after his departure his phone calls had all but stopped. Maybe if I were to see him again I would gain enough clarity to enable me to move forward on my own. On the second night, I rang Kouji's house. It came as no surprise that he was unhappy to learn I was in Japan, but he did agree to make the trip into Tokyo "*itsuka*"—sometime.

Expecting nothing from Kouji, I hung up the phone and dialed someone else, someone I could always count on. Ya-chan was thrilled to hear that I had returned and wasted no time setting up a date for the following evening.

Yuki was invariably curious about my relationship with Yasu, and sometimes I wondered whether I had become her real-life soap-opera queen. The morning after my rendezvous with Ya-chan, she was quick to ask how it had gone. I had left the house in my wardrobe finest, a royal blue Evan Picone dress and heels.

Yuki was in the kitchen drinking coffee when she asked me about my night out and how it had gone with Ya-chan.

"It was fine," I told her somewhat cryptically. "We went for a drive."

Yuki held her small cup in both hands and blew on it to cool the coffee. She looked up at me and asked between blows, "Just a drive?"

"Well, we stopped in a pub and then took a drive over Rainbow Bridge. It was nice."

I lied. It wasn't nice. It was humiliating. Just two hours after being picked up, I was in a train station restroom removing my shredded stockings. Yasu had taken me to a park to view the illuminated bridge from a distance, and there he had wasted no time removing the barrier to his pleasure.

"He keeps coming back," Yuki noted. "Don't you think he really loves you?"

I refrained from going into any detail about the evening—how I had tried to look classy but ended up being treated like a tramp.

"It's not like that, Yuki. Half the time I don't understand him...and I'm sure he doesn't understand me. Mostly we just live in the past."

My sister returned to the kitchen counter to procure a fresh cup. She poured, added a bit of sugar, and calmly sat down and blew steam off of the top.

"Kouji called last night."

"*Yuki!*" I exploded, miffed that she had not disclosed this immediately.

"He said he would call again tonight...something about coming here this weekend, I think."

Kouji arrived at Shinkoiwa station wearing his signature tight jeans and a leather baseball jacket. I was glad he wore familiar clothes because otherwise I might not have picked him out of the crowd. His hair was shorter, and his eyes were empty black stones. He was anything but the free-spirited guy who had been staying in Michigan. His rebel earring looked like part of some a façade. His girlfriend, mother, company, and society had their grip on him. It was so obviously over, but unfortunately Kouji was too weak to put it into words.

The next day, carrying a light backpack, I took a train to nowhere, picking a random line until it came to the end. From there I boarded another random train and rode it until it too stopped at its final station. From there I walked until I found a bus stop with a single student waiting. When the bus pulled up I boarded it.

As the number of passengers dwindled and dusk fell, I asked an older couple whether they knew of a place where I could spend the night. They said that if I would get off at the next stop they would point me in the direction of a bed and breakfast.

I ended up at a *minshuku*—a private home willing to take in a stranger for a small fee. After shivering all night in an unheated wing of a dank farmhouse, I shouldered my backpack and begin to walk toward higher elevations. As I headed uphill, however, it appeared as though I had stayed in the last village on earth. The incidence of houses thinned, and the only vehicles that passed were little, flat-nosed farm trucks. The road had narrowed to a single lane.

As I neared the peak of the small mountain, it began to snow. I opened and closed my hands continuously to keep my fingers from going numb.

Trudging upward, I was overcome by memories of my days on Sado. I went through extremes, sometimes laughing at myself, only to have my brief amusement transform quickly into a profound sadness, my tears flowing unchecked once again.

Eventually I passed an abandoned house, the windows broken and the papers doors tattered. It was like viewing a smaller version of Jinzo ten or so years into the future—a time when potentially no one would be around to care for the estate and the place would fall victim to the elements and neglect. My guess in the present situation was that an elderly person without relatives had passed away and that the house had been left to rot. I wanted to see the inside.

Entering the rundown shack, I was surprised to find that it still contained a number of personal effects. From the kitchen I peered into the main room, where the floor had rotted in several places. In the corner was a display case with several wooden dolls and other souvenirs.

I wanted to cross the broken tatami and take one of the dolls, but as soon as I stepped into the room the floor creaked and I became spooked; retreating, I took only a small teacup from the kitchen. I dipped the cup in a nearby stream and drank from it; having become accustomed to roadside vending machines, I hadn't expected to run out of resources.

The road leveled out for a brief stretch and then crested, after which it began a gradual descent. Eventually I came upon a hot springs bathhouse, where I paid 500 yen to warm up. After another forty-five-minute walk I entered a village and caught a train north. This ride took me to Nagano city, where I stayed the night in a business hotel. The next day I headed south, traveling through Kouji's hometown without bothering to stop.

On the fourth day, I dragged my sorry carcass back to Tokyo and confined myself to the room Yuki had lent me. There I wrote free-verse Japanese poetry nonstop for days, filling a college composition book and then some. Channeling my favorite philosopher, Kierkegaard, I became melancholy and deep, thinking about how I as a single individual existed in the world.

By the time I emerged, it was almost Christmas. I had been in Japan for more than a month doing absolutely nothing other than moping about and driving Yuki crazy. I could tell she was just about fed up with me as I told her what I had been doing in the room.

"There is something wrong with you," she assessed. "I think you are losing your mind."

I couldn't argue with her.

"Do you realize that you cry and laugh in same sentence? Nobody does that on a regular basis. It's strange."

I reflected on what she was saying and conceded that it was true. And then, based on the same logic I convinced myself that I might actually still be sane. As I sat there ruminating, Yuki continued, "And my son, Nobu, is confused. He doesn't understand why you are here without Gorgeous and Great. It is scaring him. He thinks I might leave him or something."

I felt horrible for causing Yuki so much trouble when she was trying so hard to do her best for Nobu under very difficult circumstances. I knew time was running out, that I had to figure out my life—and quickly.

On Christmas day I called the children. I had been calling them every week, but the conversations were invariably strained. Right kept us on the speakerphone and monitored every word—probably warranted, given my erratic behavior. This time Right had set up the children to attack me about having taken them out in my parents' truck—we had driven a short distance to a store, all buckled together instead of using two cars with everyone properly restrained.

Gorgeous began, "Mama, why did you try to kill us?"

I didn't know how to respond to this poignant question. *What in the world was she talking about?* I asked her to explain.

My baby went on, "Remember, Mama? When we went to Grandma and Grandpa's house last summer and we used the truck...all of us rode in the front and we had to wear the seatbelts together? To-chan said we could have died and that you tried to kill us!"

This was Right's logic.

"Yes I remember...we went down the road to the grocery store. It was just a short trip."

Gorgeous was crying and angry. "But Mama, we could've been hurt! We could've died! Why did you do that to us?"

Suddenly their father cut in. "Are you stupid? *You almost killed our kids!*"

I begged Right to stop, but he refused.

"I love my children," I protested.

Right snapped back, "*Ha!* You are a *terrible* mother!"

I asked to speak to Great.

Right refused. "You owe me money! You get a job and pay me for the kids! You pay me—then you can talk!"

With that Right slammed down the receiver. I dialed again, but no one picked up. The next day I did two things: I called Kouji and instructed him never to a call me again. Then I applied for an English teaching job in Tokyo. For the time being I would stay there and gain some working experience. At thirty-two this was my first real job.

Yuki forewarned me that landlords generally didn't like foreigners and that I'd have a hard time finding a place to rent. This was a shock to me. Evidently I had been sheltered on Sado and blind to many things. But evidently this was true. Only a handful of advertisements in the Tokyo English newspaper read "We will accept foreigners!" or "*Gaijin* okay!" I likened these taglines to ads in the United States indicating that pets were allowed.

From Yuki I learned that many of these apartments were in *gaijin* ghettos—home to "club hostesses" from other parts of Asia and Slavic countries who had come for the high wages they could earn entertaining Japanese men. Half joking, I wondered whether a special security deposit would be required lest I piss on the tatami mats.

I was determined not to live in a foreigner house but to find an all-Japanese apartment and rent it on my own. I knew there was a real estate office down the street from Yuki's, and I decided to go on my own and inquire.

Sliding open the front door of the office, I called out. A middle-aged woman answered my call from another room. As soon as she saw me, however, she stopped cold. Before I could ask about availability she informed me she had nothing.

I countered her statement. "Nothing available?" I asked rhetorically. "That's strange. There are several advertisements in your window display. Surely those rooms are for rent, or you wouldn't be showing them."

"Oh, those must be old," the agent replied evasively. "We don't have anything now."

I wasn't offered a seat, but I took one anyway.

"Listen to me," I insisted. "I was married to a Japanese man for twelve years. I can read your posters, and clearly you have rooms for rent. If I were to walk to those buildings, would I not find those rooms vacant?"

Realizing she was not going to get rid of me that easily, the lady came down and sat at her desk.

"Well, the truth of the matter is that most of the landlords will not allow me to show you an apartment. They don't want foreigners. I can't make them rent to you."

"I've heard this. But you can tell the owners I am not a *gaijin*. I am starting a teaching job in a couple of weeks. I need an apartment, and I'm not leaving until you agree to show me one. Aren't there laws against discrimination?"

Speechless, the woman offered me a cup of tea and rice crackers. She said she would make a couple of phone calls—no promises, but she would try.

Within an hour I had been shown several six-mat flats with baths. In the end I chose a second-floor corner unit in a small building that had a total of only eight units. It was only a short walk to the train station and had good sun exposure for drying laundry outside. The cost was $600 per month, a $600 deposit, and a finder's fee of another $600. I could rent it as long as I had a Japanese guarantor to back me.

My assigned school was part of a large chain that owned small academies across the country and promoted itself through TV ads as the "study abroad in front of your train station" English school.

Every day I taught seven structured lessons to groups of three and led one "drop-in" session of free conversation. I taught five days each week at my assigned school and substitute-taught on weekends at other academies all over Tokyo.

It was demanding work that required a strenuous output of creative juices to get through the day. I never knew who was going to show up for my classes, and I had to make every combination of students work well together. The job kept me on my toes; I had to be "on" every day—which for me, ironically, was like therapy. It was "go, go" all day long, and by the time I got home I was mentally spent.

On my days off, which were rare, I would walk randomly in one direction or another. I'd walk for hours with a map in my hand, navigating the winding streets until I grew tired, after which I'd turn around and try to find my way back by memory. If I didn't feel like walking I'd go to my favorite fancy goods shop and buy a jigsaw puzzle. In this way I stayed out of trouble.

Sundays were the designated day for me to call the children. In a private agreement with Right, I was informed that I could speak to them as long as I paid him $500 a month. On Mondays I sent them letters written in Japanese, always sending along trinkets like trading cards and stickers.

None of this made up for my being so far away for so long, but this was all I could do at the time. I didn't know how—or even if—I would ever get my children back. A court would never award me custody under the circumstances, and they had changed mentally—their malleable brains had been turned against me.

Beyond the calls and letters I tried to avoid thinking of my children. Frankly, such thoughts made me want to jump—to step off train platforms, hurl myself down flights of stairs, or leap in front of a car.

Every now and then when my mind got away from me I'd call my old friend, who would come by and comfort me. Our crazy relationship—whatever it was—had developed into a somewhat healthy friendship. About every other week we'd hang out, drink a little Suntory whiskey, and watch TV. Sometimes he would stay over, but this was rare.

As stipulated in our teaching contract, teachers couldn't take time off for the first six months. It was a joke among Nova instructors that our school name stood for <u>NO</u> <u>Va</u>cations. After exactly six months and one day I boarded my regular flight back to Detroit.

The children were attending a summer program at their school, about thirty minutes from the airport. A Mazda wife picked me up and drove me there.

As we pulled up to the schoolyard, I could see them both immediately. Gorgeous, in her plaid jumper skirt, stood next to a teacher, looking out over the other kids—perhaps looking for me, I decided, wondering when I might arrive. Her little brother was roughhousing with some boys.

I got out of the car and walked slowly toward my daughter, who didn't see me until I was within about ten feet. Upon spotting me she was overcome with emotion.

"Mama, Mama! It's my *mom!*" she screamed as she pushed forward toward me. Throwing herself into my arms, she declared that she had missed me.

I was overwhelmed by Gorgeous's reaction. Over the past few months she had been cold on the phone, and I hadn't expected her to be glad to see me. Now, though, she was quite literally shaking.

Holding my daughter close I scanned the playground again for Great, who had heard the commotion and was walking slowly toward me. Although it was only June, his face was bronzed from the sun. His father had given him a bowl haircut, and he was missing both front teeth. To me he appeared a foot taller.

"Great! It's Mama!" I called out. "I came to see you!"

My son appeared frozen. He had always been the clingier of the two, but now he seemed shy. After a few minutes, Great did approach, and we hugged. I pulled out a few small presents from my carry-on.

"I have more in my big suitcase," I promised. "I'll bring them when I come back in a couple of days, okay?"

My parents had arranged for all of us to take a little camping trip together. During our short reunion this morning Gorgeous stayed close to me. She had so many troubles to share: no one liked her at school, her father made her watch her little brother all the time, and Great almost never obeyed her. She had earned "student of the month" at her school, receiving a nice certificate for her efforts, but Right had forced her to tear it up and throw it in the garbage because she wasn't working to her potential. Worse than this, he had pulled her out of Japanese school, having deemed her incapable. More than once he had made her stand outside in the dark of the cold Michigan winter for hours so she could feel what it would be like to be destitute—"homeless like stupid people," as he had expressed it. He was taking these extreme measures to push his daughter to do her best—harsh but imaginable from the perspective of the culture in which Right had been raised.

As Gorgeous described the details of her home life, she was almost hysterical, begging me to return to the house and save her from her father's strictness. Unfortunately, I had no ability to do what she was asking, but in retrospect I should never have returned to work in Tokyo. Vocationally, I should have accepted whatever else I could have found with my philosophy degree and household Japanese. I should have been closer, even if that had meant dealing with Right head on. Gorgeous at only eight was bearing the brunt for my absence; he was demanding everything of her.

It was painful to witness my daughter's reaction, but I didn't know how to stop her father. I couldn't just walk in and take the children back. A fight would ensue, and under the circumstances I would invariably lose. Right had a good job and a comfortable home to offer, and it was he who had been caring for the children. His disciplinary measures would be seen as harsh, but in comparison to my actions the lesser of two evils.

At the end of the vacation, I dropped off the children at their house. As soon as Right opened the door, their demeanors changed from somewhat uninhibited to robotic. His first words were a barked "wash your hands," to which they responded in unison *"wakarimashita"* (understand/understood) as they stepped into the *genkan* and their father shut the door behind them.

PART III

Disentangling

CHAPTER 13

Soba or Omelets?

On my own as I lived and worked in Tokyo, I became increasingly cynical. Most nights after work, I'd find flyers advertising schoolgirl videos shoved into my mail slot. Each title featured a headshot of a girl with an indication of her age. It was during this time that I became familiar with the term lolikon, *derived from combining the French word* lolita *with the English* complex. *To be a* lolikon *meant being attracted to prepubescent girls—being into "erotic cute."*

In a culture with ways that had at first seemed so gentle and refined, something had gone terribly wrong. Mothers were obsessing about their sons' success to a degree I'd never seen in the States, and family expectations ostensibly dictated the need for a fantasy outlet. I couldn't stand getting on a crowded train filled with businessmen because I couldn't help imagining what was behind their eyes as they pored over their weekly comics. I was taking my first baby steps toward returning to the person I had been before Japan.

OUR SCHOOL WAS AN AVERAGE size Nova with seven teachers on staff. Countries represented were the United States, Canada, and Great Britain. While the other teachers were somewhat fresh—just out of college and new to Japan, in my early thirties I was the elder stateswoman of the crew. A ragtag bunch, many trying to pay off student debts while gaining international

153

experience, we taught students from all walks of life—from businessmen to housewives to school children to the occasional retiree. I began to mentally categorize them.

The way I saw it there were three groups of women, defined by age: schoolgirls, young wives, and middle-aged mothers. Behind their dark eyes I observed signs, things they didn't talk about in any of our open conversation forums.

The schoolgirls knew the routine. Outside they acted cute and idol-like, pretending to be innocent—which entailed trying to look and act a bit younger and more naive than their years—while at the same time hiking their skirts on the way to school, using a hidden belt, in order to add a touch of sexy mystique.

Students of around my own age, young wives who had perhaps looked up to the '80s idol Matsuda, Seiko, were undoubtedly doting mothers in the background, anxious to ensure that their children, girl and boy alike, enjoyed equal opportunity—while all the while clearly distinguishing "fighter hero boy" from "cute innocent girl" and thereby unwittingly pushing a helpless, submissive nature upon their female children.

Then there were the middle-aged women, ladies who reminded me of Satoko. Typically taking English as a hobby, they were relaxed and happy, responding well to instruction. For them learning English was an escape from their placating, worry-filled lives centered around their oldest child—particularly if that was a son.

When it came to male students, we had a large population of businessmen who came after work, along with several younger men who attended regularly. Many of these were interested in learning English for travel, as well as, of course, for their future careers. Right or wrong, I lumped all Japanese men together as dirty-minded and potentially pedophilic.

We teachers were assigned three students at a time in any combination, as long as they belonged to the same skill-level group. For any one class, I could be assigned pupils from one or more of my four stereotypes, and as one might imagine, with protocol almost always being a factor in Japan, certain combinations could be challenging to manage.

It happened that one day I walked in to one of the worst combinations imaginable: a low-level class consisting of two middle-aged women and a man I estimated to be in his mid-twenties. The young man probably assumed he would have his way with the lesson, but I was determined to manage him.

From the get-go, as predicted, Toshi set out to dominate the group. When he asked the women their ages as part of the icebreaker exercise, I immediately called time out, explaining that Mrs. Ando and Mrs. Suzuki were young, beautiful women and chiding him for asking such a thing.

In response the young man rolled his eyes as though I'd said the most ridiculous thing he could imagine and proceeded to try again. Turning toward one of the women, he asked, "Are you a housewife?" Mrs. Ando affirmed that this was indeed the case, but afterward I pounced on Toshi again.

Looking him directly in the eye, I clarified, "She is a manager. She manages her home. Can you ask the other lady if she is a manager as well?"

The student was taken aback. "Do you discriminate me?" he asked in broken English, evidently assuming I was picking on him.

"No, I do not. Are you discriminating against them?" I asked, using grammar that was several lessons beyond his ability. "Why don't you ask them if they are engineers or businesswomen? Don't think older women are always housewives."

Throughout the lesson I continued to struggle with the young man. I was known as a fairly strict teacher with a rather dry sense of humor, and though most of the regulars seemed to understand and appreciate my hard-driving style and desire to impart Western culture as part of my lessons, I had to curb my drills for the sensitive ones.

As Toshi got up to exit the class, he called me a Communist and then made his exit without stopping at the front desk to book his next lesson. He was scheduled for a second class with another teacher, but it appeared that he was finished for the day. In the student's file I wrote, "This one is a little psycho."

I worried that Psycho would file a complaint against me with the office staff, but that didn't happen. I kept my eye on his file, periodically pulling it out and checking it for activity. After a two-month absence he returned without explanation, appearing at the door of the teachers' lounge with a cassette tape. Indicating that it contained his original heavy-metal compositions, he asked whether I would be willing to give them a listen and provide him with feedback. This was a peace offering.

During the next few weeks, Psycho scheduled private lessons with me, which required him to "purchase" all three seats in the class. In a private lesson I wasn't required to follow the regular nine-step lesson plan. It was up to the student to drive the lesson; he could opt for a normal lesson, work with me on English homework, or request free conversation. Psycho invariably wanted to discuss two favorite topics: his music and the Czech Republic.

Toshi claimed to love all things Czech, much as I had loved Japan. He had studied political science at a good university and had been drawn to Eastern Europe following the collapse of the Berlin Wall. I knew nothing about these places but explained that I had fallen in love with Japan years earlier and understood how this could happen. I advised him, however, not to look outside his own country for happiness.

Toshi didn't heed my advice. One day as I was on my way to teach a class he waved me down. He had apparently applied for a job with a tourist agency in Prague some time earlier; now, with an offer on the table, he planned to live abroad and had come to tell me he'd be leaving soon. I wrote my phone number on a scrap of paper and slipped it to him, hoping for an opportunity to talk to him about his fascination with a foreign country. Contact with students outside class was forbidden, but I wanted to hear about his plans and perhaps dissuade him.

A couple of days after giving Toshi my number, I was at my six-mat drinking whiskey with my old friend when the phone rang. I spoke Japanese in an effort to steer the conversation quickly to an end. Toshi was taken aback by my fluency, accusing me of not being a real foreigner and of intentionally trying to fool him. Ignoring this comment, I instructed the young man to call another day, telling Yasu that the call was from a student who was leaving for Europe soon and was interested in some extra lessons.

The next night was one of those lonely, binging nights when I couldn't stop thinking about my babies and feeling like the worst human being on the planet. It was then that the phone rang. I agreed to meet Toshi at a convenience store and from there walk with him the rest of the way to my place. Immediately upon seeing me, he could tell I wasn't the same confident Nova teacher he had come to know. I was incredibly down, and he could sense it.

When we arrived at my place, Toshi pressed me to tell him what was wrong. In slurred Japanese I tried to explain: "I had beautiful two children, and I lost them! It is completely my fault. They live a very hard life with their father because of me. Can you imagine my guilt?"

I went on to explain how my family had taken Yuki in for a summer and how I had then come to Tokyo and found everything so cool and wonderful. I told him about Right, my babies, and my life on Sado and in Michigan. He was utterly taken aback. I explained further how I had been blind, absolutely naïve about the culture, certain aspects of which were making me somewhat bitter. I used all of this as a lead-in to talk to Toshi about his plans to move abroad and his fascination with Eastern Europe.

As we continued to talk about his plans to move and why I thought he shouldn't be so negative about his own country, the telephone rang for the second time in as many hours. I picked it up, knowing full well who it would be. "Stacy...love you!" were the opening words.

"Oh, stop joking with me! Go to bed and rest," I chided.

"Maybe I'll stop by tomorrow night," Yasu suggested. "I know it's Friday, but I can't wait until next week."

"You know I work late." I said trying to send him a message.

"Oh, I see. If tomorrow is too bothersome I'll wait until Friday. Let's make it Friday," Ya-chan mumbled, trying to save face.

"*Hai yo*" ("Yea, sure"), I replied, imitating his favorite line. "Now close your eyes and go to sleep."

For once I was taking care of him over the phone. Perhaps he'd had a bad day at work. After hanging up I turned to Toshi and offered an explanation for the strange exchange: "An old friend...a drunkard."

Awkwardly Psycho moved toward me and held me in his gangly arms. He asked to stay the night, and I allowed it. I was lonely, tired, and too drunk to care either way.

The next morning I woke up late. It was already 9:00 a.m., and a student was lying next to me. I was scheduled to teach at 10:00 a.m.

"Hey!" I called out in an imperious tone. "Wake up!" I poked at Toshi. "Tell me you don't have classes today! Tell me that!"

"I have lessons today. I have to use up my lesson package before I move to Czech," he informed me as he rolled onto his back.

"Ahh, crap!" I said in English. "You don't have a private lesson scheduled with me, do you?"

Toshi affirmed he had two lessons booked with me in the afternoon, which I promptly asked him to "no show." After he refused on the grounds that he needed to use up his lesson package before moving to Czech, I tossed him the keys to the apartment and asked him to lock up.

My stomach was churning when I arrived at school, and I was sure I smelled like liquor. Running into the teacher's lounge, I checked the posted schedule. I had Psycho slated at 1:00 p.m. for back-to-back lessons. The timeframe was highlighted and marked "Special Request." At that point I thought I should begin a little acting job.

"Dang," I exclaimed to the other teachers in the lounge. "I have that crazy psycho Czech student again."

"Oh, Toshi?" the younger Brit, Claire, asked brightly. "I think he's lovely."

"He never follows instructions. All he wants to do is have free conversation, and you know what the headmaster thinks about that!"

The other young Brit, Jane, added her two cents: "I personally think he's attracted to you. He keeps on scheduling sessions and requesting Stacy specifically."

"Oh, stop! He's such a pain, and I'm just a mother figure providing advice."

"Well, I wouldn't mind it if a tall, handsome man like that had a crush on me! I think he's the best looking student at the school."

The girls were practically gushing as we each prepared for the onslaught of students that would begin before 10:00 a.m. We talked about swapping classes so the Brits could have a crack at wooing Toshi, but the headmaster overheard us and leaned in to the lounge to remind us that there were no trades.

Predictably, my afternoon back-to-back lessons were a disaster. The open classrooms felt like fishbowls, and at one point Toshi leaned forward to pass me my apartment key, laughingly informing me that he'd had to use a kitchen towel for his bath. I raised my voice to ensure that the headmaster could hear: "Now, Toshi, you keep forgetting that you must have a 'be-verb' in front of the action verb with 'ing.' Let's practice!"

Shortly afterward Psycho's job offer in Prague fell through, and within weeks he casually spoke of wanting to marry me and perhaps someday moving to the United States. Having become jaded when it came to the culture—and specifically to Japanese men (*with the exception of Yasu, whom I still considered to be a close friend of sorts*)—I should have run from such a suggestion, but I didn't.

Toshi was none of the things I had come to hate about Japanese men. From his interest in me as an older woman, and based on opinions he shared regarding the exploitation of young girls, he was a breath of fresh air. He respected my mind and was willing to shoulder some of my baggage. He talked easily and shared many of his thoughts aloud, so I could trust him more than I could my old friend, who tended to be more quiet and complex.

In short order Toshi took me to meet his parents, who were educators as Satoko and Hideo had been. Unlike my ex in-laws, however, they were much more progressive and open. Although I have no doubt they had plenty of reservations about our situation, Toshi being their second son of three they appeared to have no "chonan" expectations; their sons seemed free to live their lives without undue burden.

Toshi secured a job with a nonprofit advocacy company for the mentally challenged, and soon afterward he and I were wed at the city office and moved into a 2DK (two rooms with a dine-in kitchen). During this time I returned to Michigan twice to see my babies. The first time I was given a few hours with them in a local hotel room; the second time only my son came out to eat lunch with me.

It wasn't long after that last trip back home that Satoko called. This was the first time I had heard from my ex mother-in-law in more than two years, and she began the call with accusations that I had stolen money from their son. I assured her that everything had been agreed upon in the divorce and that additionally I had been sending monthly payments to Right. I offered to send her the records, at which point she abruptly switched topics.

"What are you doing in Japan, anyway? You were such a good mother, and we believed in you!"

"I love my children. I wish I were with them now," I responded.

Right's mother continued, "When you were in Sado the last time, it was obvious you had changed. When I gave you money to buy a new dress, to change your look, you knew at that very moment you were going to leave Right, didn't you?"

I admitted that this had been true. "I had completely lost myself. You know how Right is. I couldn't take it anymore."

My ex-mother-in-law breathed a judgmental "ah-ah" with sharply rising and then falling intonation, after which she gave me some marching orders.

"You have to go back to Michigan," she told me. "You need to be near the children for support. They need you."

I was surprised at her request. From my experience, custody sharing was rare in Japan. Even if the parents lived in close proximity one or the other party generally dropped out of the picture completely. I had assumed this was the way the house of Jinzo preferred it.

"I want to go back," I agreed. "And I will."

Satoko added, "I'm glad you are paying money. You should pay. Now go back to Michigan, and help when he asks for it!"

After that phone call I began to seek work back home. My Japanese had improved greatly as my exposure had increased, but I wasn't sure it was good enough for any real job dealing with a Japanese clientele, as would be natural, given my experience. In any case I thought my best bet would be to become an interpreter, as philosophy majors were not a hot commodity in the job market.

In April 1997 the news was filled with stories about the "Little Girl Murderer" Miyazaki, Tsutomu. I watched with particular interest the old footage of his apartment following his arrest in 1989. Inside were stacks of sexually graphic anime, horror films, and child pornography. The case details, and particularly the killer's motives, were of special interest to me.

I often ranted to Toshi about how wrong all of this was, insisting that sexually explicit and implicit anime and videos involving underage-looking girls should be banned, that taking photos under a girl's skirt wasn't at all humorous, and that parents in Japan were putting far too much emphasis on their sons' success, driving them to perversion.

A month after the murderer was sentenced, five months after Satoko's call, I secured a translator position in the same small town where Right had landed his first engineering job, two hours from Detroit. In a simple phone interview the vice president of an automotive supplier offered me work based on my promise to secure several texts on Japanese manufacturing and study in advance of my first day on the job.

To me Japanese was always fairly easy to speak, but reading and writing the language were other matters because of all the Chinese characters (used for the past twelve hundred years by the Japanese as part of their writing system) one had to learn in order to be literate. I had been stuck at a sixth- or seventh-grade reading level for quite some time, and what I was being asked to do to prepare for my new job took every bit of my free time as I painstakingly looked up hundreds of new characters and technical words to get through my assignments.

In May 1997 I returned to Michigan with my second Japanese husband. Toshi secured a material planning position with another automotive supplier, and we purchased a small house with a couple of acres on the edge of town. Great, a third-grader at the time, was willing to stay with us every Saturday night, and Right wasn't opposed, as long as I did all the transporting and helped our son complete his Japanese school homework. This meant almost no quality time beyond the daily rigors, but we did our best to make the most of the little we had been given. Gorgeous refused to even talk to me on the phone, let alone visit or stay at our home.

My work as an interpreter/translator was interesting. I worked in a large, open room with many Japanese and American engineers, all of whom were male. The job entailed tagging along behind the Japanese in the factory, helping them impart their manufacturing wisdom and bolstering their confidence when it came to their relationships with American managers and workers.

In the course of this work, I often heard my ex-husband's name mentioned in derogatory tones. Mazda was a huge customer of our company, and Right had caused plenty of trouble for our quality team, holding the components we manufactured to impossible standards and harassing our managers about minor details. An American engineer shared with me that Mr. Chrysanthemum Pond of Mazda had at one point practically taken our company down. Although I couldn't verify the truth of that assertion, I could only imagine that Right was an ogre and a thorn in everyone's side. *For what it was worth, though, I felt certain that the cars produced by the Flat Rock plant had high quality exterior trim, meeting every specification to the letter.*

Outside of work my greatest joy was having Great visit. Into my second year back he not only spent every Saturday night with us but also many weeks in the summer. Little by little he began to divulge secrets about his life in Detroit.

Great was still being beaten with the bathroom towel bar whenever he failed to obey on some minor point, which to a degree I construed to be "old-fashioned discipline"—more common in Japan than in America at the time. But it was the more subtle things Great divulged that scared me. He was often forced to sit at the dinner table for long periods of time to complete homework while his sister and father "napped." During these confinements he wasn't permitted to leave the table until his father retrieved him. Great shared that he had snuck away from his chair a few times to listen at their door and had gotten the impression they weren't really sleeping. To him it sounded as though they were involved in some sort of wrestling play; my son reported strange noises from beyond the door.

It was all I could do to keep myself from marching over to Right's house and confronting him; instead I called the Wayne County Child Protective Services and requested an investigation. When an interview of the children in Right's presence yielded nothing but strict parenting, I insisted Gorgeous be interviewed once more at school. This move completely backfired, further alienating my daughter from me.

I worried that Right might not allow Great to visit us following my intervention, but apparently Right's need for a break from his bothersome son outweighed his concern that Great might rat him out again. Finally, when

Great informed me that he had been locked in a bathroom while his father and sister went to dinner and a movie, I decided the time had come to make a move. I hired the best attorney I could find in Detroit and began custody proceedings for my son. My lawyer advised me that my chances of getting Gorgeous without her consent were practically zero.

In December 1999, the court ordered that Great move in with Toshi and me, and together the three of us lived rather happily, freed from weekly commutes to Detroit and the burden of completing that crazy Japanese homework. Great made new friends and assimilated quickly. Once every month or so I would take him back to Detroit to visit his big sister. Intensely bitter that I had taken her little brother, she would barely glance in my direction. I had saved one while completely losing the other.

Over the next couple of years, I became a skilled technical interpreter, working for two different companies. During the course of this employment, I learned a great deal about the now wildly popular "lean manufacturing"— a term coined in the United States after Toyota had imported its version of Japanese manufacturing to the United States when it joined hands with GM in a cooperative venture to build cars in California in 1984. Since "lean" is at its core a philosophy, and since it involves the structured application of certain rules and principles, I naturally responded to it and was able to teach others.

Over time I became the mouthpiece for the corporate CEO—not to mention the first female manager in our global organization. I prided myself on providing thorough explanations, incorporating all of the context I had gained in Japanese life up to that point coupled with my understanding that Americans needed more words to conceptually grasp what they were being asked to do. It was my job to read the minds of Japanese men and provide Americans with the whole picture.

Despite the gaping hole in my heart regarding Gorgeous, life was relatively smooth. Great was adjusting to his neighborhood and school, and Toshi and I were working hard to get ahead...but all was not well with me. My cynical resentments against Japanese men had a way of showing themselves at work, and I often wore my emotions on my uniform sleeve. When an important, multi-facility conference was held at our factory the male managers, both American and Japanese, dressed in special white jackets, while I, the only female manager at the time, was instructed not to sit at the table but to stay out of the way behind the Chairman.

This was a simple enough request, requiring the standard "Yes, I understand" response, but my attitude quickly spiraled downward, and I was asked to leave the company. Although there were thirteen other Japanese companies in our town, I had no desire to work for any of them. I was no longer willing to be their girl Friday.

Toshi was about to become an innocent victim of my mental shift. The fact of the matter was that my husband and I had evolved into an economic unit—sleeping in separate rooms. He still wanted to live in Europe and pursue music, while I desired to stay in Michigan. When an American company in another town expressed interest in my Japanese manufacturing knowledge, Great and I made the move, leaving Toshi behind. It was as though I'd become tired of my drug and wanted to put some distance in between myself and it. After five relatively successful years together, I filed for divorce from Toshi, and that was that.

With this move I entered the final stage of my *bonsai* life, becoming the addict who quits but expects to continue using socially. For the most part it was my plan to leave Japan behind, but sometimes—maybe once a year or so—travel there on my own to see Yuki and my special friend, who at thirty-seven remained unmarried and was invariably willing to see me.

Ya-chan and I had often discussed a "Same Time, Next Year" sort of arrangement, meeting up for a liaison once a year—something I'd seen in an old movie starring Alan Alda in which star-crossed lovers, each married to a different partner, met up on the same day at the same time every year for a brief tryst. No matter what happened in our lives, I imagined that after everything else this would be our fate.

In the fall of 2001—Thanksgiving weekend—it was *Mouichido, Mouikkai* (One more time, once more). Yet again I boarded a plane for the past—a short weekend in with Ya-chan.

It was like old times: the same intense intoxicating feeling, followed by a terrible withdrawal. Late on the second day, I lost all sense of place and slipped into the bathroom, where I drew a hot bath.

I sat in the water until it grew cold, and after a while Ya-chan came to see what had become of me. Whiskey in hand, he sat naked next to the tub, watching me for a while without saying a word. Finally he took his left hand, placed it on my head, and pushed me under the water. I didn't fight.

Finally Ya-chan released me. As I sputtered and gasped for air, my old friend parted my hair and looked at my face, which he was holding with his right hand. From the glass he held in his left hand he took a swig before finally speaking. "Stacy, what is in your head about us is unrealistic. This is Japan. Japanese have expectations of their sons. They tell me to get married and make a baby. I'm thirty-seven years old, right? I have to do it soon, or I will not have peace with my parents."

"Is there a girl now?" I asked.

Ya-chan looked at me with wide eyes. "There might be. It is very selfish of you to ask after everything you've done regarding us."

I admitted that this was true. It was absolutely *jibun katte* (selfish).

Ya-chan rattled the ice in his glass. "All I can do is keep you in my heart as someone who was significant in my life. Isn't that enough?"

Tweaking the end of my nose, Ya-chan smiled. "Hey…just forget about it. Dry off and come into my arms."

Ever since I'd been flying to Japan on Northwest, the meal just prior to the landing at either Detroit or Narita had been a choice between an omelet and soba noodles. I had always taken the buckwheat noodles, but on my way home I ordered the omelet tray. Having reached my absolute rock bottom, I knew I'd never go back to Japan again.

CHAPTER 14

Sailor Moon

It had taken me six years to extricate myself from the coiling wires that had shaped my life—but in order to allow my trunk and branches to straighten I had to all but completely break free from the compact vessel of Japan, leaving all its influences behind, including any objects or people who might tempt me to return and use yet again.

I HAD BEEN AFRAID OF losing my identity after my divorce from Right, but at this point I found myself in a new place, both mentally and physically. It didn't bother me that the nearest Japanese karaoke bar or authentic restaurant was nearly two hours away. I looked in the phone book for Japanese names and found only a couple. *Good!* I thought resolutely.

Over the next few months, my Japanese karaoke music CDs and poetry books gathered dust. I quite literally forgot Ya-chan's phone number and address. In fact, whenever I traveled across the state to buy Japanese ingredients for dishes I still prepared at my son's request I felt uncomfortable. Japanese men creeped me out, and the women struck me as enablers. I was stereotyping, of course, but it was good for me to keep a safe distance from something that had both been so alluring and had caused me so much grief.

I had been hired to help a small UAW shop revitalize its training program and implement some lean manufacturing on the side. When I took inventory of how things were running in the American plastics company, I realized that in their condition they were ripe for bankruptcy or a takeover and asked myself *How are they ever going to survive an economic downturn or crisis?* The company was more than a little "chubby." The Japanese managers had invariably told me "No spend!" but my new employer assured me that I could purchase any training materials I wanted, "No problem!" I was unfamiliar with such lack of discipline!

As I tried to pick my way through the processes and to research what was needed on the training front, one of the operations managers was apparently plotting to make use of my skills on the production floor. He came to my door looking for help with a particular assembly area that was fraught with defects and filled with scrap.

Walking around the line, I pointed out several clear violations of "lean": subcomponents sitting around in quantity, taking up space; associates having to detour around a spare drill they kept on line just in case their regular equipment broke down; and piles of finished goods being stacked and restacked on a long table that wasn't even needed. The waste seemed endless, but when the manager asked whether I thought I could fix the problems I told him "Absolutely!"

Although "Kent" was several years my senior—and superior to me in position and manufacturing experience—he was respectful and acquiesced to me when it came to formulating a plan. Together we trained all three shifts in lean, worked on a new line layout, and finally one Saturday carried out the transformation with our team of associates.

During the physical movement of equipment and the subsequent cleanup, Kent was on task, moving about quickly, like an agile thirty-year-old—dropping to his hands and knees to scrub the floors and equipment until they shined. He reminded me of my father, and I was struck by the effortless quality of our working together from the moment he had entered my office door. We made an excellent team—our styles were both similar and complementary.

It was on that very day that I realized how silly I had been to go so far—to the other side of the earth—to find a place I could call home, when all along I could have stayed close to the place of my birth.

Even though Kent was a good-looking man, tall and blond and with a disarming smile, I had all but ignored these fine qualities in the course of my work. I had never dated an American guy and was tired of men in general. But by the end of the transformation Saturday, as we were both standing around—filthy, tired, and satisfied—I saw something very special in this man. His lead-by-example ethic and sense of humor had won me over. Apparently he felt the same.

On the following Monday our work together continued. The workers on the line needed to get used to the new flow and pace, and it was our job to help them adjust and troubleshoot any problems as they arose. As the day wore on, it became obvious that the two of us were going to have to sit down and talk.

Pulling Kent aside, I told him without embarrassment, "I think I'm attracted to you."

Kent admitted what I already knew: that he felt exactly the same. My response was a huffy *"That's just great!"* and with that I stormed out of the factory. I was actually hoping he would tell me I was nuts—to make things easy on me, but he didn't. I knew the trouble such an admission would bring, as Kent was married with two younger children.

Kent admitted that he had been unhappy in his marriage for some time, and from my side I had no scruples. Blinded by adoration and unable to bring ourselves to remain apart, against better judgment and healthy morals, he moved in, left his wife, and married me, in that order.

In the beginning the situation was a bit awkward in that I was accustomed to keeping up my Japanese husband radar. In the past I'd paid a great deal of attention to Right and Toshi, continuously on the alert for any hint or nuance that they just might be in need. Not surprisingly, Kent found this unnecessary, deeming my propensity to say "I'm sorry" completely over the top. Little by little I grew accustomed to speaking my own mind and began feeling like an equal partner in the relationship. Within a year or two I found my voice, to the extent that even Kent may at times have been a little overwhelmed!

Not only did I get to think and speak freely, I was able to get back to some of the activities I had enjoyed as a child. An avid outdoorsman, Kent took me fishing frequently, on small inland lakes, rivers, and the big lake—Lake Michigan. Together we bought small cabin in the north woods where we enjoyed all kinds of outdoor fun, including my longtime favorite, snowmobiling!

All was well with our daily lives, with the exception of the ordinary tribulations one would expect in situations dealing with the fallout of broken homes, but Kent and I worked hard together to make our circumstances work. Each of us (especially me) had taken grave missteps in our lives; now, for the sake of our children and ourselves, we were all about avoiding unnecessary turmoil.

The damage to Gorgeous appeared to be irreparable. During her middle-school and high-school years, I would only see her in passing, when she and her father would pick up Great for a short trip to Chicago or to travel abroad to Europe or back to Japan. I had all along been assured by consoling family members and friends that one day when Gorgeous grew older she would see teenagers around her having fun and eventually break free from her father's controlling grip. I waited eagerly for that day.

Finally, at the end of Gorgeous's senior year there was indeed a small breakthrough—in April 2008 I received an invitation to attend her high-school graduation. After all her father's pushing and as the result of her own hard work she was graduating at the top of her class, having achieved the position of valedictorian. I knew that this had been neither easy nor natural for her to accomplish. She had very likely driven herself crazy studying in her quest to prove to Right that she was not stupid.

On the day of her graduation, I stood in line with Right waiting to take a seat. It had been a long time since I had even spoken directly to him, but we were cordial—mutually happy over the occasion. Like any proud father who was into photography, he carried a large camera, along with a bag of equipment, to capture the moment.

Gorgeous proudly led the processional, and as she marched I couldn't help but recall my little Sailor Moon—my tiny, wand-waving heroine—and her apparently God-given determination to succeed almost from the moment of her birth. Despite having had to deal with two cultures, a demanding father, and my abandonment, she had made it.

In that moment I breathed a sigh of relief. Surely the unspeakable acts I had suspected for years had been a figment of my overactive imagination—a cultural mix-up combined with a young child's confused perception of some completely innocent moments of affection between a father and his daughter.

Following Gorgeous's graduation I hosted a small family party in her honor at a park near the town where I had grown up. Shortly thereafter my maternal grandmother died, and Gorgeous came to the funeral to honor her. Three times I saw my baby in a very short period of time. I even received a call on the morning of my birthday. *Maybe*, I dared hope, *just maybe she is finally breaking free.*

But just when I thought everything was on the mend, the *daruma* came back to teach me a lesson. Long ago I had made a very specific wish but had been too impatient and untrusting to wait. The much belated results of that behavior were about to be revealed—the consequences of my defying gravity, of forcing things to happen before their time and against good reason. *The floor was about to drop out of our oh-so-close-at-hand happy ending.*

Like those crazy carnival rotor rides that spin so rapidly the centrifugal force leaves one stuck to the walls as the floor drops two or three feet, our lives were about to spin so wildly out of control that all we would be able to do was to let ourselves fall.

It was the day before Thanksgiving 2006—less than two weeks after Gorgeous had called to wish me a happy birthday—when she called again, this time catching me at work. At first when I heard her nervous voice I thought, *She's going to tell me to go to hell—that her recent contact with me had been a mistake.* But this wasn't at all the case.

My heart stopped when I heard her voice. *Go ahead*, I thought, wanting to get the inevitable worst out of the way. *Give it to me. Tell me you hate me and that you never want to see me again.*

"It's my dad. I'm having a lot of problems with To-chan."

Gorgeous's voice was loud and forceful; my reserved, always in control daughter was practically yelling. My first thought upon hearing these words was that my baby's newfound independence was causing friction in the house. Perhaps they were fighting about things Gorgeous wanted to do—about teenager stuff delayed.

"What's going on, baby?" I asked. "Are you fighting with your father?"

Gorgeous paused. "I don't know how to say this, but…I found a camera hidden in the bathroom…in a bucket…and there was a hole in the bucket… pointing at my shower."

Time stopped. My hands shook, and I couldn't speak.

"Mom, are you there?" Gorgeous asked, concerned.

"Yes, baby, I'm listening…go on."

"This time he went too far, Mom. I found a camera before…a few years ago…and I told him to stop. He promised, but he did it again. I'm thinking about turning him in to the police…but I don't know what to do. I'm scared."

It was surreal. My mind was racing to the point that I could barely process what she was telling me. Huge tears dropped onto my desk as my daughter continued.

Gorgeous continued, "My friends…um…I told a couple of people and they said I have to tell the police or the evidence will be gone. They said I have to act *now!*"

It was incredibly hard to process what she was saying; it was coming at me so fast I couldn't get my bearings, couldn't force my mind past my denial. Gorgeous was saying something about a camera in the bathroom…about evidence. *What on earth was going on?* As strained as our relationship had been, I thought I needed to proceed with great care.

"Baby, I need an hour or so—can you give Mama that?" I managed to ask. "I'll call you back in little bit. I just need time to think."

"*No, you can't call me!*" Gorgeous screamed. "I'm using a friend's phone right now because my dad checks everything. He looks at my phone every day…times my driving."

Of course he did. He always had to have complete control.

In the end we decided to correspond by e-mail. Before she hung up Gorgeous gave me a stern warning not to call her father for any reason. I assured her that I would do no such thing and promised that, whatever was going on, I would be behind her 100 percent.

I hung up the phone and drew a ragged breath. Sitting in my chair unable otherwise to move, I resorted to bouncing my legs up and down and wringing my hands. *He had promised—had said he would never do anything like this… had sworn that the photos and comics were part of a fantasy world and that father-to-daughter adoration was natural and common. Either he had lied or his views had changed.*

Over the next hour, as I thought through the possibilities of what had already occurred and what might happen next, I came up with a plan—the one I thought would be easiest on my daughter. Fearing that legal action might be too risky, that Right would be released on bond, pending trial, and do something completely crazy, I suggested in my e-mail that I take possession of the evidence and make Right an offer he couldn't refuse. Maybe if I threatened to expose his actions—to go to the police—he would agree to return to Japan and stay there.

A few hours later Gorgeous replied.

Hey Mom. I have pictures of me in the bathroom as evidence. They are contained in a memory stick. I also have the camera. The question is how much longer can keep I these things without him knowing they are missing? It's very hard for me to get the evidence to a friend's house because he might suspect something. A friend from high school has offered me a place to stay tonight, and I can stay as long as I want, within reason.

My dad is not going to agree to go to Japan. He wants to keep me. Therefore I feel that negotiation with him will not work. He is just going to get violent. There have been countless times when he became violent and tried to keep me by threatening me. Do not call him until you have permission from me.

Gorgeous

The note ended with no real indication of what might happen next, but when I got home Kent was already in motion. His plan was to get Great out of town—to take him north—and hunt while I sorted through the terrible situation unfolding in Detroit.

The next morning a little after eight the phone finally rang. Gorgeous informed me that she had an appointment with a detective at 11:00 a.m. and that a friend's mother would be taking her there. With this I jumped into my car for the three-hour drive.

Gorgeous appeared strong when I walked into the station lobby—clearly more ready to confront the situation than I was. Following a preliminary interview with a police officer, we were led to the back of the station, where we were introduced to a detective who seemed rather agitated.

"I had to leave Thanksgiving dinner, and I'm not sure why I'm here," he opened rather peevishly, obviously skeptical of whatever he'd heard thus far. I looked him in the eyes.

"Sir, this girl has been waiting many years for this day. She just happened to be ready on a holiday, and she can't wait another day."

Frankly, I had no idea of exactly what Gorgeous would say. I didn't know what had happened for sure, but she did have the memory stick—the one from the hidden camera.

As we sat there Gorgeous told the detective about the physical abuse she had long endured at her father's hand, how he had habitually slapped and kicked her. She described how he had flown off the handle, becoming jealous, when she had mentioned a boy she liked at school. She told him about being verbally abused, repeatedly being called stupid, and how her father controlled her every move. She also talked about her father's obsession with a girl named Kelly. Apparently he had practically set up Gorgeous to befriend the girl and had in his possessions albums upon albums of pictures he had taken, both with her knowledge and from afar.

Right's infatuation with Kelly reminded me immediately of his early obsession with my sister. How horrible for Gorgeous to have been forced to endure not only her father's lusting after her but his advances toward her friend.

With each sentence Gorgeous's tone became more and more aggressive. Years of pent-up memories were pouring out of her. While every example of her father's abuse was truly horrendous, I became concerned that the acts she had so far described would be insufficient to put him away for long. I spoke up.

"Ah, honey, is there something more you need to tell the detective? Have you said everything?" I coaxed.

Gorgeous bit her lower lip, looked down, and shook her head from side to side. With this the detective asked me to leave.

During the time I was sitting with Gorgeous, her phone rang several times as her father tried to reach her, and when I returned to the lobby Kelly's mother—the mother of the girl with whom Right had most recently been infatuated—claimed that her phone had been ringing as well. With Right's permission Gorgeous had stayed at their house the night before, and they had driven her to the station.

After a couple of hours of pacing and looking out for signs of Right's arrival, I was brought back to sit with my daughter. This time the detective had a few questions for me.

"Ma'am, does Mr. Chrysanthemum Pond have guns?"

I replied that I didn't think so.

"Is he into martial arts?"

I told them that Right was a third-degree black belt in Judo, though sorely out of practice.

"Will he be able to understand our commands?"

"Yes," I answered.

It was 4:00 p.m. when the search warrant arrived. In the meantime additional officers had been brought in, and we watched as they suited up in their combat gear. We were told that it might be a long night and that we should step out and get something to eat.

Less than two hours later Gorgeous received a call. We were to go to the house to meet the detective. Right had been taken into custody.

Walking up the driveway past the police cruiser, I noticed how untidy the front garden appeared. Years earlier, after my departure, Right had transformed the lush green lawn into a version of his father's garden on Sado. All that remained of that grand showpiece was a bunch of overgrown trees and bushes; in comparison to the other houses in the neighborhood the yard looked terribly unkempt—almost eerily so.

Stepping inside for the first time in many years, I felt as though I were walking into a museum crossed with a crime scene. *This must be*, it occurred to me, *what it felt like to enter a place that had been transformed from the location of a private tragedy into a public display.* Many furniture items were sitting just as I had left them, but all around was significant clutter: unopened shopping bags and mail littering the tables and floor and children's school artwork from years earlier haphazardly taped to the walls.

Gazing out of the back window into the backyard that I'd kept so manicured, I noted that all of the tall hardwoods had been cut down and remained left as they had fallen. Around the dismantled trunks and branches weeds had grown tall. The fence we installed brand new and the jungle gym Right constructed for the children by his design were dilapidated and falling. The only things still standing in the entire yard, in fact, were two towering evergreens. The seedlings I had planted for my children alone appeared to have thrived.

After inspecting the contents of the house per the detective's orders, Gorgeous was asked to sign a release. Three pages of items had been taken into evidence, including cameras, computers, and albums. The detective commented that he had never seen so much pornography and that highly suspicious materials had been removed from a false ceiling. When I asked about Right, the officer told me he had been arrested without incident.

We were asked to stay in town for the weekend, during which there were multiple trips to the station for interviews and updates, as well as a trip downtown to the county prosecutor's office. In the meantime Gorgeous and I would stop at the house and do what we could to put things in some semblance of order. After surveying the contents of all three floors, I came to the conclusion that Right had lost all control.

Although the police had taken many albums and CD-ROMs, there were many more strewn about the house. In the basement above Right's exercise equipment, hung a poster-sized picture of young girls running in a park. Included was Gorgeous's friend Kelly. In Right's bed I found a hand-knitted winter scarf in a feminine color, which Gorgeous identified as Kelly's. Her father's dream, she shared with me, had been to marry Kelly to save her from all the "bad guys."

From the time of my arrival at the station on Thanksgiving Day, I had been careful not to ask Gorgeous about the content of her allegations to the police. She had avoided giving the detective any detail in front of me, and it was obvious she wasn't ready to talk. Finally, on the second night, after tossing and turning, my daughter abruptly sat up and began to let it all out.

Right had begun to nap with our daughter shortly after my departure—when Gorgeous was just seven. Little by little, in this manner he had groomed her. By the time she was eleven the abuse was full blown, and he had often bragged to Gorgeous that taking her virginity was the best thing he had ever done. At the moment of this disclosure, my worst fears for my baby's safety were realized.

The next morning we went to the police station one last time to learn about the next steps in the process. We were met by the detective working our case, along with one of the county prosecutors who had interviewed us the day before. They sat us down at a round table.

Gorgeous looked at the prosecutor. "Are you keeping him in jail?" she asked urgently. "He has to stay in jail. I can't go to school if he gets out of jail." Her voice had once again become extraordinarily loud.

"Yes, we believe he will remain in custody. He has given us a complete confession. We have everything on tape. The ages match up. It all fits together. We have him."

Before asking the detective for details, I turned to Gorgeous and gave her a high five.

"He was very upset—concerned about his daughter. We told him you were here taking care of her."

I wanted to know whether Right was remorseful—whether he even seemed to realize that what he had done was wrong.

"You know…I'm not sure he believes that what he was doing was wrong. He's a sick man, and he's going to do some serious time."

What the detective didn't know was that Right wasn't a typical pedophile, that the kinds of materials in his possession were perfectly legal in Japan, that little girls as young as Gorgeous had been when her father had first molested her were considered sexually erotic by a certain proportion of the male population in that country—a population large enough to support a fairly large, open market industry. No, Right was hardly an average American pedophile, someone who hides behind closed doors in shame; he was much closer to the average Japanese pedophile. In Right's case he had taken his fantasy too far in a space he had thought was safe, within the borders of a country that wouldn't tolerate this behavior.

The last question the detective had for me was important because Gorgeous's safety at this point was everyone's first priority. He asked whether I thought Right might be a flight risk if he were to find the means to escape. My answer was an emphatic yes! Right had access to plenty of funds; my concern was either that he would flee or do away with himself.

"I'll note that," the detective responded. "His bond hearing will be next week."

"Detective?" I had a question myself. "Will news of this arrest be released to the press?"

"I'm going to try and prevent that."

I could picture the headline: "Mazda Exec Being Held on Molestation Charges."

"That would be best," I agreed.

Part of me wanted the general American populace to view some of the ugliness that happens behind Japan's paper doors, but this would have been devastating for Gorgeous.

Despite my strong suggestion that Gorgeous come back with me and start a new school near our home, she refused to consider it. Finals were on the horizon, and there were papers due. She never missed school. And so because her own house had become in her eyes a detestable, poisonous thing, she opted to stay in a high-school friend's mobile home until we could find an apartment.

As I dropped her off at the mobile home, all the strength I'd mustered to get Gorgeous through the weekend had been expended. Leaving her with strangers in an unfamiliar downriver neighborhood, after having held my daughter close for days, was hardly something I wanted to do. Even though I was saying good-bye for only a few days—until I could get back the following weekend to help—I could take no more. As the door closed behind my daughter I broke down and sobbed inconsolably.

The day after I returned to the west side of the state, I phoned Mazda HR to let them know them know that Manager Chrysanthemum Pond would not be returning to work and to ask how long Gorgeous could continue to drive the company car. We were given a couple of weeks, the time required for Right's absence to be considered job abandonment and the paperwork to be processed before the two cars provided as part of his compensation package would be retrieved.

On Tuesday we received word that bond had been denied and that Right would indeed be held in jail. This was a tremendous relief, as Kent and I had thought through what we would do if he were to be released. Thankfully Gorgeous was safe and could complete her semester.

Over the next few days, I could hear Right's screams in my head—echoing screams I imagined bouncing off the hollow walls of his cell. The man was in complete denial—hoping beyond hope that this was all somehow a mix-up—that his actions would be seen as natural for a man and a young girl who loved each other and that his daughter would somehow want him back. Thankfully, there was just enough of the American in my now-grown daughter to know better.

CHAPTER 15

Dead Trees

Consequences aren't always immediate. The fallout from poor life deci-sions can rain down over years, decades, and even generations. This rain is not the replenishing kind but acidic.

"IT'S JUST FANTASY," HE HAD told me. I should have known better! I had promised myself then that I would never accept that part of Japan, but I had passively allowed such nonsense to exist in my own space by failing to run from Right and leave Japan immediately after I had realized the full impact of my discovery.

I was furious inside, angry beyond belief or the possibility of relief. To verbalize aloud "My daughter was molested" was difficult enough, but having to mouth the words "My daughter was a victim of incest" made me physically ill.

Thanksgiving weekend 2006 was in many ways the worst of our lives, but the damage had been done over time, over so many years. Now, hopefully, we had finally turned the corner. I was thankful Gorgeous was no longer under her father's direct control and relieved that Right remained locked up.

Because Gorgeous's school was a commuter campus, no dormitories were available, so finding an apartment was imperative. It was Gorgeous's preference to stay in the downriver suburb where she had spent most of her memorable life—if possible, she wanted a place near the security of the police station. Even though her father was in jail, where we were assured Right would remain, Gorgeous was nervous and afraid, continuously looking over her shoulder. Every evening at precisely 9:00 p.m., I talked my baby down from her nervous ledge of fear, a fear that she refused to share with any counselor for fear of being someone else's fodder for voyeurism.

Right didn't have anyone to take care of his business in a crisis situation—no family nearby and no real friends outside of work—so it was up to me to manage all of his affairs, and that included notifying "next of kin." According to Gorgeous, Right was in the habit of phoning his mother every Saturday. Hideo had passed away a year or two earlier, but Satoko still lived in Jinzo. Two weekends went by before I mustered the nerve to make the call. Because I feared that the shock of what I was going to say might quite literally kill the old woman, I chose to get in touch with Right's sister first.

Naomi was completely aghast when I told her what had occurred—disgusted and angry with her brother. Deeply concerned as well about her niece, she sympathized greatly with our situation. She also lamented her own. Already shafted when her brother had ditched Jinzo and his *chonan* responsibilities, she would now have to figure out how to manage the stigma of his essentially disappearing from the face of the earth. Before this the family had always been able to fall on a response like, "Oh, Right? He's an engineering manager for Mazda in Detroit." *Now* what would she say?

The day after I had spoken to Naomi, Satoko called my house. The conversation was awkward. My Japanese had become rusty, and the words I needed to draw upon were buried deep.

"Oh, that boy...Right...Why, oh why...did he do this?" she cried out almost incoherently.

In that moment I felt sorry for Satoko. Hers, it seemed to me, was a fate close to death. Her son was imprisoned in another country, and she would likely never see him again. How could I respond from my position?

Satoko continued, "When Right came to Sado last with the children, I told him to keep more distance from his daughter—that he paid too much attention to her."

She had seen it—the very things Great had sensed she too had intuited.

"But Right...Oh, that selfish boy...You know we purposely tried to keep him from coming to Japan for his own father's funeral? We were afraid he would make a scene...like he always does for everything."

I expressed my sympathies.

During that call my ex mother-in-law lamented many aspects of Right's behavior but also expressed concern about her son's situation. Then she asked about Great.

"I suppose Great will live with you, then? He's in high school, so you will need to take care of him."

What? I thought. Apparently she'd been kept in the dark.

I explained that Great had been living with me for more than six years. Right had taken both children to Sado once in between and had apparently kept the change of custody a secret.

By the end of the call, I knew the old woman better than I had ever known her before; the real Satoko had come out in her very failure to ask about Gorgeous's condition and state of mind. Naomi had surely explained the nature of Right's crimes to her mother, but not once did she ask about my daughter's welfare. This, in my opinion, rendered Satoko completely unfit as a grandmother to my children.

Following my conversation with Jinzo, I reached out to Yuki by e-mail. Always busy with her career, she rarely responded to my annual mailing of New Years cards, but somehow I knew this update would awaken her. She expressed shock over Right's actions and seemed deeply concerned for Gorgeous. Yuki, my dear sister, had been somewhat in the dark about my circumstances since my meeting Kent, but as I filled her in on the life I had been living since giving up Japan, I think she recognized that I was no longer on the verge of insanity—that I had attained some level of stability, post-Japan.

While we all waited tensely for Right's sentencing, Gorgeous and I spent many weekends together cleaning up her childhood home and rebuilding our relationship, which was awkward and precarious. There were times when we laughed—for example, whenever we unearthed *another* of Right's Carpenters CDs filled with sappy love songs (there were about fifty of these, all told, scattered about the house). At other times, when memories became too much, we would both break down.

Disposing of Right's extensive media collection took the longest. The police had confiscated a couple of trunks full of material, but there were still a good many mysterious homemade CDs and albums containing pictures of both Gorgeous and Kelly. We took the time to shred each photo and break every CD, making absolutely certain they would be unrecognizable to anyone who might rummage through the trash.

Many of the albums included more typical pictures—beautiful likenesses of my daughter and her friend taken at various school events over the past several years. Of these, Gorgeous wanted to retain only a few. Thinking about who had been behind the camera and what he may have been thinking in the moments he took the snapshots marred in her eyes anything lovely about them.

Among Right's things I recognized a stack of laser discs as ones he had purchased from a small appliance shop while we had been living on Sado. Among them I recognized two anime laser discs I had never personally viewed. On a whim I decided to grab the player and the stack of video albums and take them back home with me.

The first disc was a futuristic, coming-of-age tale featuring a young boy and girl. Their encounters gradually led to sex, for which the young girl was embarrassed and ashamed, but the boy eventually became her hero and their relationship thrived. The second disc, set in prewar Japan, was the story of a motherless girl forced to perform sexual acts on her powerful father, a military official of some kind. Taking both discs outside, I broke them in half and dumped them in the trash.

Over the next couple of months, Right wrote me several letters from the jail. Much of the content consisted of instructions regarding the house and his financial affairs. Because these issues did need to be managed and the sentencing had not yet occurred, I accepted his mail. Interspersed among tedious instructions about this or that, however, were instructions regarding our daughter. Right was essentially advising me to dismiss what he had done. He expressed the belief that Gorgeous shouldn't carry the burden of feeling bad about what had happened between them—that the two of them had shared a beautiful bond and that she shouldn't listen to any therapist or counselor who might tell her otherwise.

Gorgeous was unwavering in her testimony against her father, conveying her sentiments in a sobering victim's statement that was read at Right's sentencing four months after his arrest. Aware that she had struggled with language (both Japanese and English) since she was a small child, I could only imagine how her unfiltered words must have affected Right as he listened to his own behavior described in quite vulgar terms. Because the physical evidence was overwhelming and Right's confession matched what Gorgeous had told the police, Right was encouraged to plead guilty to two of the many counts against him. In April 2007 he was sentenced to serve a minimum of ten years for first-degree criminal sexual assault and possession of child pornography.

Gorgeous had been trained to study—*to study as though her very life had been at stake.* Having stood outdoors on several cold, dark nights as a punishment for failing to try hard enough, my daughter had been engineered to be a studying machine. In some ways it was this dogged determination to succeed that had carried her through. At any given moment she was much too busy preparing for that next test and writing that next paper to think about breaking down and losing it. Certainly she dealt with posttraumatic symptoms—always somehow mitigated by that next looming paper.

Outwardly Great took the news of his father's incarceration in stride, as he did most things. Having endured a childhood characterized by abuse and disappointment, he seemed surprised by nothing. His initial comment at the time of Right's incarceration had been one only a jaded teenager could have made. "*Really?*" he'd asked, followed by, "*If my dad was going to prison, at least he could've gone for something cool....*"

Nearly a year later, the sale of Right's home complete, all of the details were technically in order. I had both of my children back, along with the love of a man I considered my true soul mate and a good life that included plenty of outdoor activity. During this period I considered all of these, taken together, my key to happiness. But I was wrong about this...as wrong as on the day I'd pinned all my young hopes on living in Japan and becoming Japanese.

In 2006 all the prayers I'd offered on the altar of culture had come crashing down on me: the reverence I'd shown faceless gods, the penance paid to ward off evil, hope placed in papier-mâché dolls and tissue monks. All of this meaningless nonsense no philosopher could defend. That "rock bottom" I'd hit years earlier when I'd known for certain I'd never again "use" Japan as my drug of choice had been redefined by Gorgeous's revelation. As horrible that was, it was unclear to me now whether what we'd just endured was really the end of the story or whether there was more to come.

CHAPTER 16

Idols

Once upon a time I'd stood in front of Jinzo's modest barn wood tem-ple and studied the offerings placed in the roadside lean-to by passersby. Interspersed among weatherworn stone Buddha statues had been seem-ingly random objects—coins, a boy's hat, and that crazy, naked blond baby doll, her face scribbled with blue. Now it seemed as though I had become the foreign doll standing among faceless gods. My only hope, it oc-curred to me, was to think my way out, to put the pieces logically together so as to prevent further damage.

I WAS GUILT RIDDEN AND sleepless. Night after night I tossed and turned, wor-rying obsessively about my children, no matter how well they seemed to be doing. I was always on guard—trying to protect them both from the demons I had known and from those I hadn't yet met.

Being deliberative was key. I had to be able to predict failures and protect them from negative consequences. Many would say I was too late, and of course I would agree, but this was all I could do for them at this point. My mind was on double duty, trying somehow to make up for those years I'd been physically absent.

My consternation was primarily focused on the future, but at the same time I couldn't let go of the past. No longer mesmerized by culture, I could chronologically see the chain of events stretching back behind me for what it had been and understand some of the driving forces behind what had occurred.

Looking back on our individual lives, my upbringing, Right's childhood, and various chance events that had intervened, the writing had been on the wall. But for me there was one missing link: How much of what Right had done could be attributed to Japan itself—to the culture I adored?

I wanted to put together a case—not a defense, but an explanation. It was too late for us, but was there anything to be learned from what Right had done? At the risk of sounding cliché, if I had this piece of the puzzle, just maybe the record of our situation could be of use—help someone else before it was too late.

I had begun my adventure with very limited insight. It's difficult today to think back to a time when information about foreign places came via the evening news, teachers, and library books. People born in the '60s, '70s, and earlier couldn't access the resources we have today. Common views were more generalized. The Soviet Union and Red China, for example, were stereotyped as evil Communist countries, and we knew that there were those in places beyond our borders who committed gross injustices and honored less than savory practices and customs.

Thirty-five years ago, thirty-five years after the Japanese had surrendered, in 1980 the once "evil Japs" had acquired the reputation of being exceedingly clever on the basis of their rapid postwar turnaround. Although we had a few bones to pick with our new ally over international business practices, the Japanese were otherwise viewed as fine people; no one had thought twice about my going there.

Nor should they have. The only strange-seeming practices talked about at the time were old—prearmistice, really—things like the "kamikaze" bombers, ritualistic suicide by sword (*hara-kiri*), and blinding nationalistic tendencies that had driven this nation to declare war on just about everyone within their reach. Those days had passed.

Still, in retrospect there was something about Right that had gone beyond his family's brand of nurture, beyond his having been written off as a "bad seed." I was no anthropologist, but I wanted to know whether Japan's national character, past or present, was driving Japanese men to idolize and objectify young girls. Further, I was curious about the validity of Right's claim that collections like his own constituted mere fantasy in the eyes of Japanese men. *Were child molestation rates higher or lower in Japan than in the United States? What about incest? And if the rates were higher, was the* lolikon *culture to blame?*

These are matters I couldn't have researched in the 1980s and '90s, when I was at the height of my addiction. The information simply wasn't available. But the situation is vastly different today for the culturally curious who have at their fingertip, disposal to an all-access pass to exploring and learning about people and places. Google anything, and one can find plenty of information, some of it fact-based and much reliant upon perspective. Japan and I had been intimate for a long time, but I didn't know whether we were unique in our situation. Was anyone else out there talking? The answers to my curious questions about Japan's "little girl idol" fascination were likely just a few clicks away.

Googling the issue in 2009, though, proved to be a less than satisfying venture. My initial search, "incest in Japan," yielded some unexpected results. Apparently, unbeknownst to me I had been living in a country where "mother-son" sexual relations were, if not common, at least thought to be useful in some situations when a male child was struggling to focus on his studies. Besides this there were articles on familial bathing and sleeping arrangements; I was familiar with both, though we had practiced neither in our home.

My next entry was "pedophilia in manga" (Japanese comics)—which, I was certain, would provide me with plenty of resources. Surprisingly, the result of my search was disappointing. It seemed as though the majority was blind to what I had noticed so many years earlier. In fact, the couple of bloggers who questioned the content of Japanese comics (*wondering whether they were really seeing what they thought they were!*) seemed to be ganged up on—sent to blogger hell for their negative impressions of what clearly constituted free speech and art rolled into one.

The closest I came to discovering someone else calling out the Japanese for pedophiliac tendencies was an article by a travel writer using the moniker "Road Junky." This individual wrote: "Japan is about as kinky as sex around the world gets. Cute doll-like girls and frustrated salary men, love hotels, and pornography everywhere."

The blog author went on to describe many of the same issues I'd become aware of during my time living in Tokyo, centering around the way school-girls were idealized, depicted in comic books as sex objects—as the subjects, difficult as it is to believe, of erotic fantasy to the point that there were vending machines that dispensed the used panties of schoolgirls.

In my view Road Junky's description of Japan's kinky infatuation with young girls was 100 percent on the mark. If only her blog had been available to me before I had first traveled to Japan, before I'd become so head over heels involved that I might have thought twice. At the very least, my eyes might have been opened sufficiently that the minute I realized Right had me speaking and dressing much younger than my age, I could have taken off running.

But from all indications, I may have arrived on the shores of The Land of the Rising Sun just as this toxic "cutie culture" was ramping up. Apparently it had begun with idols like Matsuda, Seiko—a girl my own age who was quite possibly the idol I'd seen singing on TV that day I'd first arrived at Yuki's house. Her adorable ways would be mimicked by future pop singers and then by impressionable young girls watching from home. This would in turn feed the comics and anime.

Finding no fact-based postings to satisfy me, I turned to a source I thought would be more reliable: academia. Searching for an expert, I located an anthropology professor at a prestigious US institution who was the author of several books on Japanese pop culture. I composed an e-mail to her describing my experiences: how I had discovered the "Petit Tomato" photo collections in 1986, how my husband had explained his fascination with the images as innocent fantasy, and how in the end he had made his dreams reality. I closing I made a request:

Japan's acceptance of adolescent girls as sex objects needs to end. With this nearly impossible mission in mind, I'm looking for someone in academia who has studied incest in Japan, lolikon materials, and the mainstream acceptance of prepubescent girls as sex objects. Any subject related to this is of great interest to me.

The professor, who was kind enough to reply, seemed to support my assertions, but indicated that her research had taken her in other directions. Her primary focus, as I understood it, was *moe*: a fascination and even an obsession with fictional characters who could potentially be sexual in nature. Her response included these words:

(My colleagues and I)...try to be sensitive to how fantasy works in a realm that doesn't necessarily translate to the so-called real world. But I also know that fantasy impacts life and am not surprised that there would also be pedophiliac repercussions.

The "so-called real world"? I thought incredulously. *What, precisely, did that mean? And weren't the repercussions serious enough to have been studied already?* I in turn responded:

It is so beautiful to think the Japanese could fantasize about the cute innocence of children without perverse sexual thoughts. It is amazing that any female scholar could go for this, and I'm glad you are not buying it. I think a few are culturally blind like I was.

In our case, my daughter had just enough American support to realize she could come forward. She knew the system here would support her, and there would be no shame on her American side. You can imagine how such a crime would quickly get covered up in a Japanese family. If a girl in Japan were to report incest, what would happen to her family's reputation and her own future?

In a second reply the professor kindly suggested that I reach out to her contemporary in England, who specialized in Japanese visual arts. This new contact supported the notion that suggestive drawings depicting cute young girls were created and purchased in response to societal pressures. She further suggested that an examination of the potential risks of such escapism would make an interesting research project—but advised me that she would be unable to take it on for some time. She referred me to a third scholar in Japan, a gentleman known to be an expert on *otaku*: modern subcultures that defy Japan's societal expectations.

Although I was leery of reaching out to any Japanese male on this topic, I decided to give it a try. In a rather curt note this professor answered none of my questions about cultural underpinnings and only suggested that my daughter and I seek psychological help for what had occurred. Giving him the benefit of the doubt, I thought maybe his English was limited and I should have written him in his native tongue.

I had been hoping to find answers and support, but after these three exchanges I felt completely alone in my pursuit. While my searches produced bits of information that could potentially be pieced together into a narrative that would explain Right's crimes in light of his culture, there seemed to be no call for action coming from any authoritative source. This dampened my enthusiasm for continuing.

As I was about to put away my notes, an unusual phrase came to mind, something I may at some point have read somewhere. I typed "Japanese National Character" in the search bar. The result carried me back to my high-school library. *The Chrysanthemum and the Sword*, written in 1946 by Ruth Benedict, had been rather dry teenage reading, and I couldn't specifically recall any of the content, but I distinctly remembered the book. As I scrolled through some of the excerpts and quotes listed on the web, I stumbled upon a few sentences that coincided with my own impressions. The Japanese, she reported, are "both aggressive and unaggressive, both militaristic and aesthetic, both insolent and polite, rigid and adaptable, submissive and resentful of being pushed around, loyal and treacherous, brave and timid, conservative and hospitable to new ways."

What a dichotomy! When I thought back to my initial encounter with Japan, "polite" and "aesthetic" rose to the top of my list. Everything had been beautifully processed, ideal in form. But as I had become intimately enough acquainted with Japanese daily life to begin to experience its underside, I had begun to glimpse an aggressive, militaristic rigidity that was driving some (men in particular) to be insolent and resentful.

Ms. Benedict also wrote about Japan being a "shame culture," as opposed to the West's "guilt culture"—a nuanced distinction I found fascinating. When I reflected on my own situation in this light, I recognized that Right had never really needed to berate and shame me for my mistakes; my own desire to do well, as well as my own conscience, would alone have driven me to do better. I saw this difference as operative all over Japan, in both schools and workplaces. As an interpreter I had repeatedly encountered Japanese managers who, unaccustomed to dealing with Americans, wanted me to voice their extreme disappointment and come down hard on workers. I had found it necessary over and over again to carefully temper such rhetoric and coach the offenders.

My final Internet search went back full circle back to the beginning of the whole problem, which wasn't Right and the Japanese culture but my own strange addiction—the one that had allowed me to tolerate all of this nonsense as it had unfolded before me. I entered the key words "cultural addiction" into the search bar. In 2009 there appeared to be no recognition of such a phenomenon.

And so—because there was at the time no "Japanaholics Anonymous" dedicated to helping recovering addicts like myself, and because all I could hear were my own words echoing back in response to my cries of a "cultural foul" being committed in Japan—I set aside my research and continued with my busy work and home life.

My brief foray into searching for some semblance of logic that would allow me to make sense of the senselessness hadn't produced the answers I needed in order to find sleep. Having no way of predicting when and where the next terrible event would rear its head, I could only resort to worry.

CHAPTER 17

Fighting Gravity

When I first experienced Japan, I thought this intriguing culture held the secrets to a good life: order, process, and an almost artistic approach to everything. But my blind faith in this culture was sorely misplaced. In fact, placing trust in any culture is risky without a set of standards by which to measure the moral rectitude of any given custom.

IN EARLY 2015 I FOUND myself with a little spare time. My biggest worry—the welfare of my children, who had endured so much in their early lives—no longer manifested itself in guilt-ridden nights of tossing and turning. Gorgeous was well into her career and grad school, and Great had also made it through a tough curriculum and was employed in his chosen field. On most evenings I went to bed early and slept through the night. Kent had retired early from his factory management job and had lifted a good bit of the general household management weight from my shoulders.

It was then—just a few months ago as I write—that I found it conducive to reopen my old files. I began to peruse pages of memories I'd captured from my Japanese days, as well as the pasted links from my Internet searches dating back to 2009. Within my notes were the names of three scholars about whom I'd nearly forgotten—the experts I'd contacted in my quest for insight. As I read through my exchanges with them, I wondered whether any of them had taken up my challenge.

I pored over the pages and pages of documentation, stepping once again into the past and placing myself on Sado, inside Jinzo, and then back in Detroit. I recalled my frustration in trying to communicate, to convey to these professors and to others around me what I'd seen and done and why I thought there was something more to it all.

As I read I felt a warm hand touch my shoulder. The sensation was familiar, but it was neither Kent nor any other family member. No, it was someone who had been with me all along, someone who knew it all and agreed, finally agreed with me that it was time to tell the Tale of Bonsai (*Bonsai monogatari*).

The beginning was for me the hardest part; should I start with meeting Yuki or Right or with the accident? Sometimes, I knew, writers started with the end and then went through chronologically in flashback mode. I didn't know much about style but nonetheless felt inspired to begin typing, given my fresh understanding of the issues.

By the time I neared my two hundredth page, I felt as though I'd gained more clarity than I'd ever had before, when out of the blue a friend invited me to attend a local speaking event—a "Pecha Kucha Night" at a local brew pub. The name was curious to me, connoting as it did an old, conversational way of saying "small talk" or "chit chat" in Japanese. Evidently this was a new format for conveying a concept or telling a story within a very short period of time: in precisely four hundred seconds. I was interested, and although this all sounded somewhat pretentious and a little too "artsy" for Kent's taste, he agreed to accompany me.

As we sat and listened to each presentation, we were amazed by the array of topics and the enthusiastic support in the room. Midway through the evening, I advised my husband that I'd already signed up for the next event. Usually reluctant to share details of my past with strangers, I felt that the time had come for me to speak up.

The pressure was on. I had worked my way through approximately two-thirds of the material I intended to cover in book format, and if I could just get to the end of the story I thought I could succinctly express in a brief spoken summary the salient points of my experience for the benefit of anyone else who might be thinking of a headfirst dive into a completely different way of life. To this end I once again sat down and googled the same words I had researched in 2009, six years earlier.

On a positive note, I learned that the Japanese Diet had in 2011 banned the manufacture, distribution, and sale of nonfictional child pornography; the possession of such material was finally prohibited in 2014, with a one-year grace period provided for citizens to dispose of their collections.

Although this was terrific news, a victory for the women's groups that were leading the charge, there was in my opinion still a loophole—a particularly lucrative one being protected by a community of artists, publishers, and filmmakers. Underage fictional characters could still be drawn nude participating in sexual acts—a problem called out by CNN in a special report the summer after the law had taken effect.

In response to CNN's report, as well as of another thorough article posted by the BBC in January 2015, I expected an outpouring of concern regarding Japanese-produced comics and animation, but I found the expected public outcry to be woefully lacking. In fact, many fans of the media mocked the reports, along with the very notion that the art form should be censored.

In 2010, shortly after I'd put away my initial research, Keith Lee had published a blog article titled "The Tradition of Incest," in which he described Japan's sordid cultural fascination with interfamilial interrelations. Another find was a 2012 article in *Japan Today* by Steven Simonitch, titled "Is incest Japan's latest literary craze?" In it the writer listed twelve popular manga (comics) that featured young male characters being sexually enticed and teased by their little sisters.

I was gratified to note that correspondents and social media were at least talking about the previously taboo subject, even though the articles seemed in my estimation to be rather lightweight in terms of throwing around the blog rooms any overt condemnation of the "art."

Whatever the configuration of incestuous relationship—mother-son, father-daughter, brother-sister—none of it is "normal," nor should it ever have been romanticized as such. *Why*, I castigated myself now, *did I fail to see early on just how "okay" the idea of these falsely romanticized relationships was becoming?*

The story line of incest in Japan, I learned, is as old as the culture itself. Japanese mythology contends that the islands themselves were the children of an incestuous relationship between a brother and sister. Strange, fantastical lore, however, must be perceived as precisely that. There is no reason to accord it the normalizing power of modern forms of expression in our information-intensive world.

Kent listened supportively as I bent his ear on the topic of the Japanese media and my firm conviction that little girls *had to be* experiencing molestation in their own homes at a rate far beyond that being reported. Aware that I had volunteered to speak publically, he wondered what exactly I was planning to say.

"You aren't planning to bash *Japan* in your speech, are you?" he asked, worried. I assured him I was going to do nothing of the sort and explained that he alone was privy to the full extent of my frustration.

"You do know that the child pornography stuff you're always talking about has nothing to do with your addiction, right? You were addicted before all of that surfaced."

I fully agreed with this point but told him I was planning to bring up child pornography in Japan only as an example of what one might encounter beneath the surface of a country's beautiful exterior.

My long-suffering husband had been attempting to watch a fishing program, but I didn't care. I lowered the TV's volume to ensure Kent's full attention, and my voice became loud and forceful, like Gorgeous's always did when she talked about her father and the past.

"Kent, I became addicted to another culture and couldn't stop using it despite tons of warning signs!"

I began to list my supporting points, from how I'd noticed Right acting creepy when he first visited my house to the nude photos he wanted me to take of myself at seventeen to his comments about women in their twenties being old to his infatuation with my sister to his abuse of everyone around him to his collections and finally to everything I'd tolerated in the culture that supported his disgusting behavior.

"I wanted to be Japanese to the degree that I could ignore these things against my better judgment!" I explained, speaking in my stimulated state at an abnormal rate of speed. Finally I came up for air, and it was in this brief moment of silence that Kent interjected. He asked me what would have happened if I had gone on an exchange trip to Ireland or France—someplace "more normal" in his American eyes.

Thinking through his excellent question, I answered that I didn't think my addiction would have gotten so out of hand had I gone to such a place.

"The exotic, cool nature of Japan had me so high, so out of control. It wasn't a recreational drug; it was hardcore," I concluded.

I calculated that if I had become infatuated with a country with values closer to our own, I might have perceived a few oddities or dealt with a few "screwy" customs, but nothing on the order of what I had gone through living as the wife of a traditional Japanese man who had been twisted by his own culture.

Kent at long last appeared to understand what I had all along been trying to explain. I'd seen him feign comprehension before, just to tune out my endless jabber, but this time he looked sincere.

"And you know," I added thoughtfully. "These days everyone is tolerant, and I understand all the good that comes from the acceptance of other people and different ways, but there's something important everyone should think about."

This was the philosophical piece—the critical part: "Some cultures might be tolerant of incest, all hush-hush about such things, but does that make it okay? Does the reluctance to blame the offender or the lack of perception of guilt make it okay?"

I proceeded to answer my own rhetorical question, telling my husband I'd read that parental incest is the most damaging form of child abuse, based on the absolute control by the offending parent. Kent teased me about wearing him out, but in the end he seemed to grasp my point. Feeling victorious in my ability to finally convey my thought succinctly and passionately, I returned to my writing.

How my "chitchat speech" would turn out I hadn't a clue, but with the enlightened perspective I'd gained four years earlier, along with my newly discovered voice, I was going to give it a try.

That hand upon my shoulder telling me it was time to write was the hand of the living God. Finally, after my years of futile attempts to convey the pressing reality in my head, in 2015 God allowed this to occur. Instead of trying as I was prone to do to fight gravity, I at last allowed myself to trust Someone infinitely greater than any man-made daruma *to instruct me when to move forward.*

How was it I'd come to believe? Some five years earlier, in the winter of 2010, not long after I'd first put away my personal writings and simple research, a silly thought had entered my head, and although I'd tried to shake the notion, it persisted.

At that point one might have guessed that I was about to fall off the wagon, to purchase a ticket to Japan to indulge in my addiction yet again, but this gentle urging was something completely different from the uncontrollable need to partake of something foreign. I felt instinctively that I needed to explore a part of my own cultural heritage—a piece of it I'd all but ignored.

In our town stood a large stone church. Despite its imposing façade, I sensed something warm about it. Having passed by the building hundreds of times, I repeatedly noticed its large, stained-glass cross.

One day, having felt the need for several weeks to learn more about the Christian faith, I found myself stopped at the traffic light directly in front of the First Church of God.

I wondered to myself, *Who goes to a place like that? Moreover,* why *would someone go?* I had heard the major arguments for God in my philosophy classes—the notion that the first "cause" that made everything come into being was in fact the Creator, that perfection could be conceived only if there were in fact a flawless entity such as God, and so forth. But none of the philosophers had swayed me to believe that a godlike force existed, let alone that it could be equated with the Christian God—the One who purportedly *cares* about our sad little human existence.

It was probably these thoughts rattling around in my head—subconscious recollections of my long-ago coursework—having unaccountably surfaced that made me think about the church and those people who for whatever reason apparently believed.

Feeling too awkward to simply walk in and ask someone whether I could begin a study of churchgoers in general, I decided to begin my research where I always did: on the Internet. This time, though, instead of obliging me to follow dubious links and references, the church had an active website with pages featuring its core beliefs, events, and classes. As I sorted through the information, I found a section for "new believers" that described an upcoming class for people who, like me, were curious about Christ. Without a second thought I filled out the electronic signup form and enrolled.

My family had attended church for a period of time during my growing up years, and I had enjoyed some of the youth activities, but I had never gotten into the doctrine. Beyond this blind participation, I hadn't thought much about Christianity other than to mimic Right's position that it was a ridiculous proposition that Christ—who died like any other mortal man—could actually have been the son of God—as in God himself!

Kent claimed to be a Christian, but every time I asked him to explain why he believed as he did all he could come up with was a vapid "I just do." This didn't advance my understanding in the least. Some structured statement of reason was more along the lines of what I was looking for.

Entering the church for my first "Alpha" class, I remember thinking, *There's no way this is going to affect me. I just need to put this whole God thing to bed and move on to something else.* Telling myself I was about to attend a history class of sorts, I followed the signs to a small room where I was met by a slew of smiling faces. Having spent all day in the office, I wasn't in the mood for more chitchat and schmoozing. People didn't understand me easily, and explaining the past was far too tedious.

The leader of the study began by telling a silly Christian joke before proceeding to describe the agenda for the evening, the same pattern we'd follow for the next ten weeks or so. After dinner and conversation, there would be a video presentation, followed by more intimate group discussions. All told, I estimated the class to have twenty participants.

The English gentleman who presented the video lectures was entertaining, humorous at times in an English sort of way, and I was inclined to listen. The course had apparently originated as a way to buttress the Church of England, whose attendance had been waning.

Mr. Nicky Gumbel spoke first of his agnostic—or, more accurately, atheist—tendencies while in college but then told of his conversion after having read through the entire Bible, cover to cover, in a single sitting. I found it fascinating (a) that someone so staunchly opposed to Christianity would choose to challenge its beliefs by reading through its tome of scripture in its entirety and (b) that such an experience would have somehow transformed him into a believer. I, for one, had found any little bit of it I'd read to be difficult and boring.

At that moment I recalled having received a leather-bound King James Version Bible from a woman in California. For a few months in 2006, after the economy had taken a nosedive, I had been taking customer service calls when an elderly woman had called in with a rather trivial question. When I couldn't answer her obscure inquiry, she had begun chatting me up. Twenty minutes later I had made a new friend.

"Sally" and I had two things in common: as a child she had fished in lakes Kent and I regularly did, and she had visited Japan numerous times. When she learned of the tragedy involving my daughter she sent me the Bible, inscribing inside the cover several passages I might want to read.

Aware that my mind had begun to wander, I turned my attention back to the video lecture. Mr. Gumbel had begun explaining why it's important for individuals to decide for themselves whether or not the story of Jesus is true. If I understood his point correctly, this is critical because God has set it up that way—to prevent our being wishy-washy in our "conviction." As essentially our "uber" parent, God wants us to recognize Him for who He truly is. And because human beings over and over again throughout history had failed to do so consistently, God had sent his Son, as had been foretold. Christ was intended to be a visible sign, a steppingstone to faith in the Father. From what I could determine faith was the piece we humans had to supply—*our dish to pass at the potluck.* This made some sense to me, but that leap of faith thing was the killer. *How on earth does someone manage to hurdle such a logical chasm?*

After attending the small group discussions for a couple of weeks, I noticed that the class was filled with believers, church members who wanted to hear the lectures for themselves and share their stories with any nonbelievers who might be in attendance. By the fourth meeting, I was hearing entirely too much nonsense for my taste—clichés and insider jargon like "God knows" and "God has a plan for you."

When someone in the group made the comment—absolutely inane, to my way of thinking—that Jesus died to pay for our sins, I lost it. It made me unaccountably angry to think that a simple "forgive me" request might be all it took to erase a wrongdoing. I was more aligned with the prospect of donning sackcloth and covering myself with ashes.

I told my group, "I own all my mistakes and their consequences, right up to the end. They're my burdens to bear...no one else's."

Upon hearing this, "the plants," as I called the church members who were attending the class not so much to learn as to support nonbelievers like myself, were taken aback. My own conviction on this point was strong.

The next week one of the plants handed me a book titled *The Case for Christ*—a defense-style presentation from a journalist with an agnostic background of evidence in support of Christ's life and work examined through various disciplines and sources beyond the Bible.

To my surprise I found the book helpful. I flagged several pages and re-read many sections, but the sticking point for me remained the resurrection. The author presented the evidence for Christ's having risen from the dead in terms of multiple accounts having been written soon after the event, their authors having been imprisoned and tortured in an effort to force them to recant their beliefs, and thousands upon thousands of converts clinging to the resurrected Christ despite severe persecution.

Still, there remained a gap I couldn't negotiate without a bridge: I couldn't fathom a living thing being dead for days, rising up, and finally disappearing into the sky. To me this amounted to a "when pigs fly" sort or proposition. (*But then again, I had stated something similar when I'd first heard of facsimile machines transmitting documents to the other side of the world, and look at where we are today!*)

It was in this frame of mind that I entered my last couple of weeks of study. This was also when Uncle George died.

Uncle George was my husband's only living uncle. I didn't personally know him well, but we had for some years been spending each Labor Day at George and Joyce's cottage. They were welcoming, generous people who had big hearts and enjoyed big fun. So when we received the news we naturally traveled across the state to the northern suburbs of Detroit for the funeral.

As I sat in the chapel next to my husband, George's life flashed before my eyes via a series of photos projected on a huge screen. In the background the song "100 Years to Live" was playing:

I'm 99 for a moment
And dying for just another moment
And I'm just dreaming
Counting the ways to where you are...
...15 there's still time for you
Time to buy and time to choose
Hey 15, there's never a wish better than this
When you only got a hundred years to live...

Black-and-whites transitioned to grainy Polaroids, which gave way to clearer 35 mm prints. Finally vivid digital shots from recent years began to appear. Following the montage, one by one various speakers stepped up to the pulpit and began describing George from every angle imaginable: how he had been a daredevil, a successful machinery salesman, a great "Grandpoo," and a man of faith. Already choked up from the pictures, I found tears streaming down my face, to the degree that I had to cover it with a tissue to quell the internal sobs that were aching to materialize externally.

I realized at that moment that I was viewing the highlights of a life well lived from every angle. George and my husband's father, Henry, had been raised as strict Baptists. Their grandfather had earned his Doctor of Divinity degree at Baylor in Waco in 1920, and there was a long family pedigree of religious leadership and piety that had resulted in numerous successes in various disciplines, as well as in the aspects of life that really matter: family, friends, and stability.

As I watched the photo montage play out once more in my head, to my surprise I felt my spine straighten and my lungs fill with air. The sensation for me was akin to that moment when "The Grinch Who Stole Christmas" watches the Whos of Whoville singing despite all of their Christmas trappings having been stolen, or even more apropos, to the instant when the wire cage holding the Grinch's tiny heart breaks open and it begins to grow.

In that defining moment, I knew there were no longer any wires holding me back—that I was completely free to love others and no longer lacked the capacity to do so. My white pine nature, beginning to feel the warmth of daylight, was straining toward it.

I can say with certainty (*this is the faith part*) that in that chapel, during that funeral, the Holy Spirit enveloped me. I felt incredibly free, not free to *do* anything but liberated in the way someone feels when they recognize that they are unconditionally loved—a quality of infinite, unquenchable love not available through another human being.

As is customary after a funeral service, there was a gathering. Ordinarily at such events I felt socially awkward to the degree that I found even hand-shaking and smiling to be forced and conversations from my end superficial. Nine years after my final break with Japanese culture, I still hadn't mastered middle-class American social graces. I typically found myself, based on unshakable habit, throwing in a few nodding bows and backing out of rooms to avoid showing my rear. My "voice" on those occasions tended to be in the Japanese passive, as in "X was done" rather than "I did X." Conversing with others outside the predictable confines of a training situation simply wasn't my forte.

I have no doubt I was generally perceived as aloof, or at least unfriendly—maybe even a little crazy—but I just didn't know what to say to people most of the time. I'd seen too much to begin to explain myself. Everyone has a story, but mine was rather "out of this world." I felt certain no one could understand my crazy addiction and the havoc it had wreaked—with the possible exception of Gorgeous.

On this day, however, I was ready to put the past aside, to look people in the eyes and tell them about my discovery. I couldn't wait, in fact, to reach out to George's children with the news of what had occurred during the course of their father's memorial. Equipped with the newfound capacity that had opened up inside me, I stepped forward to share my good news with one of George's daughters.

That night after the funeral, I went to bed and prayed. I had prayed in the past, but only to a faceless, nameless god. Now I was praying to a personal, caring God—to God, the Creator. I had a lot to share with him, chiefly along the lines of how arrogant I had been to expect that I, a mere human being with limited understanding and modest sensibilities, could handle everything on my own.

I started with the very first sin I could remember having committed as a child and began to list everything else I could recall. There were minor infringements that vividly flashed before my mind's eye—lies to my parents and the kinds of things teenagers do in their efforts to gain autonomy—as well as larger transgressions so contrary to the way God designed the world to work that I could barely believe I had survived. All of the nonsense of my past came out, not in a logical way but in a vomit of confession that would only have made sense to someone with infinitely powerful communication skills. Before I had even reached the really big sins of my thirties I had fallen into an exhausted slumber.

The next few nights I found myself repeating the same itemized list, though attempting each time to tack a few more sins onto the end. Each time I would drop off to sleep prematurely, my repentance incomplete. Finally I understood: God was telling me "Stop. I've got this. You don't have to revisit those dark places."

Shortly thereafter my husband and I began attending church services together. That summer I was baptized in Lake Michigan, and I've never looked back. By doing things more or less according to what I've perceived from scripture to be God's will (*we're all mere human beings, after all, hampered by natural frailties and vices*), I've noticed that things really do work out—if not immediately or ostensibly, then overall for our good.

I've found myself able to process Right's horrific crimes through the filter of Jesus Christ, which affords me hope that he may yet experience what I still view as an unlikely conversion. (God, I've come to learn, has a way of breaking free of the boxes we in our skepticism erect around Him.) This feels like a completely satisfying perspective—one that Gorgeous and her brother have yet to embrace.

All along, I came to realize in retrospect, I'd been fighting God, ignoring what I now see as clear indicators that what I wanted wouldn't be good for me. No matter what I chose to do in my life, the going seemed to be tough, like forcing water to run uphill, defying gravity—attempting to countermand the very laws of nature and the manner in which the world works.

Imagine me, a simple girl from rural Michigan wanting to be Japanese. Me, an intensely independent child who cherished nothing more than to be outside barefoot on her grandparents' farm playing in an unstructured manner, transplanting herself into a too shallow vessel in an ineffectual attempt to morph into a demure, soft-spoken woman.

I was born a Michigan pine, a sapling lashed by the wind that crosses from Lake Michigan to Lakes Huron and Erie. But I had allowed myself to be pruned and trained in an unnatural way, not simply in an attempt to acclimate to new soil for a time. No, in an ill-fated decision to second-guess God, I had traded in my God-given sensibilities to shrink myself into an unnatural six-foot-tall bonsai.

For a gardener to fashion a miniature ideal of a tree is one thing, but for a person to try to become someone they weren't born to be—to trade in their voice and lose sight of their values, to toss away the things they love most—is a distortion of reality just short of perversion.

Each of us is given the gift of life, and we receive all kinds of input from individuals and the larger world around us, but from a hindsight perspective it all seems rather haphazard and circumstantial. Contrary to our culture's postmodern view, in the final analysis there is no such thing as "my truth" or "your truth." That kind of thinking is temporal, based on what we know using our own limited insight at any given time. There is only *one truth*, and God tasks each of us with the responsibility to identify it and live accordingly—regardless of culture.

Do not conform to the pattern of this world, but be transformed by the renewing of your mind. Then you will be able to test and approve what God's will is—his good, pleasing and perfect will. (Romans 12:2 [NIV])

ADDENDUM: LINGUISTIC NOTES ON THE JAPANESE LANGUAGE, WITH GLOSSARY

JAPANESE IS KNOWN AS A "high-context" language; that is, it uses few words to convey much. Fluent speakers of the language are expected to essentially mind read and comprehend what is unspoken. As one might imagine, this feature of the language was involved in many of my cultural faux pas.

As part of the "high context," Japanese do not use plurals (an understanding of whether a noun stands for one or multiple is gained from context. Another unique feature of the language is that words are extended (on the front or backside) to make them more formalized or polite. For example "machimasu" or "I will wait" could be "omachishiteorimasu" said politely.

There may be some confusion over how Japanese names appear within the text. Sometime I use a character's given name; other times I use "last name, first name." In schools, workplaces, and in social settings last names are normally used. When referencing someone specific "last name, first name" is common.

For those unfamiliar with written Japanese, it can be puzzling to hear that Chinese characters are used. More than a thousand years ago, when China's culture spread across the region into Japan, the Japanese picked up their writing system and since that time have combined it with their own syllabic symbols.

The translations are my own.

arigato: Thanks.
Asa hayai desu ne!: "Such an early riser!"
chanoma: Tea-drinking room; a casual room in the house.
chonan: Eldest son. Typically this is the child who has the responsibility of taking care of his parents and receives the inheritance.
daijoubu: "I'm fine" or "Are you okay?" depending on the intonation.
damare: "Silence!" or "Shut up!"
daruma: A talisman doll used for wish making.
dekai: Large.
doyo: Japanese children's songs.
furusato: Hometown, homeland (used extended family to refer to their town of origin. Often it is where the majority of their ancestors are buried).
gaijin: A foreigner in Japan.
ganbarimasu: "I will try."
ganbatte: "Give it effort!"
ganman: Suffer, persevere.
genkan: An interior entryway where shoes are removed.
genki: Healthy, well.
geta: Traditional Chinese/Japanese sandals. They are like clogs and flip flops; with an elevated wooden base.
hai: Yes.
hosoi: Thin.
iiko: Good child (girl).
ii koto: Good, good things.
irrashaimase: Welcome.
itterashai: Go and return (a greeting used normally at the door when someone departs).
izakaya: A pub.
jibun katte: Selfish.
Jinzo de gozaimasu: "This is Jinzo." (used for introductions)

Jinzo: An old family first name named used to refer to my husband's family/house since their own last name was too common in their area.

jyorenkyaku: A regular customer of a business.

ka-chan: Mom.

kibuntenkan: Refresh. To change one's mood.

Kita Wing: The name of a Nakamori, Akina song which refers to the prominent terminal at Narita Airport in Japan.

kokochi was doo: "How do you feel?"

mattakumou: Similar to "For crying out loud!"

lolikon: A person or material focused on innocent erotica. To have a "lolita complex" is to be a "lolikon."

minshuku: A private home willing to take in a stranger for a small fee.

mochiron: Of course.

monogatari: A fable.

moshi moshi: "Hello hello" (used to answer the telephone).

Moshi moshi. _____desu kedo: "Hello hello. This is _____ (...and how can I help you)."

mouichido: One more time.

mouikkai: Once more.

ne-chan: Older sister.

obaasan: Grandmother.

Obon: The period in August when people typically return to their furusato and worship the dead and attend festivals.

ohayo: (Good) Morning!

ojiisan: Grandfather.

okaasan: Mother.

okesa: A style of old folks song. Sado Okesa is the most famous among all okesa.

omachistitteorimasu: Formalized "I will await your arrival."

Oni wa soto...fuku wa uchi: "Demons out! Luck in!" An expression used during Setsubun.

ore mo: Me too.

otoosan: Father.

panya: Bread shop.

pecha kucha: Small talk or chitchat. Also, "pechakucha" is a presentation form developed in 2003 whereby a speaker has six minutes and forty seconds to speak twenty visual slides that rotate every twenty seconds.

ryojinhomu: Nursing home.

semi: Cicada.

senbeiya: Rice-cracker shop.

Setsubun: A day signaling spring's arrival according to the Japanese lunar calendar. It falls in February and is celebrated by various customs, the most common being the chasing of demons using beans.

shima uta: A genre of songs from the southern, more tropical parts of Japan. In this book it refers to a specific song popularized by the rock group "The Boom" in the 1990s.

Shinto: The native religion of the Japanese people which involves the worship of multiple gods. Many Japanese, even if they are Buddhist, also worship at Shinto shrines and have Shinto weddings.

soo deshoo: "Isn't that right?"

sunakku: A tiny, almost private restaurant/pub with personalized service (of varying kinds…).

to-chan: Dad.

tsuyuu: Rainy season.

wakarimashita: Understood or "I understand."

warui ko: Bad child (girl).

warui koto: Bad things.

yomesan: Bride of the home, daughter-in-law, or wife.

yukata: A summer cotton kimono.

yuuenchi: An amusement park.

STACY GLEISS HAS LIVED A life immersed in Japanese culture—a culture vastly different from that of her home state of Michigan. In her experience as the teen bride of a traditional Japanese man, Gleiss found inspiration for her memoir, *The Six-Foot Bonsai.*

Today the author lives a rather simple life with her husband Kent. She enjoys connecting people to Japanese culture and business philosophies through public speaking and blogging. In her spare time you can find her outdoors playing. You can reach Gleiss at thesixfootbonsai@gmail.com

Made in the USA
San Bernardino, CA
29 October 2016